Majestic
Journey

Majestic Journey

CORONADO'S
INLAND EMPIRE

Stewart L. Udall

Photographs by

Jerry Jacka

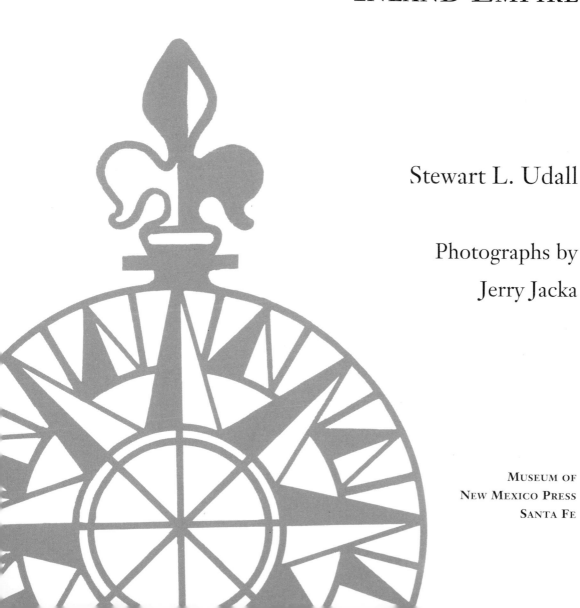

MUSEUM OF
NEW MEXICO PRESS
SANTA FE

Majestic Journey: Coronado's Inland Empire is a newly composed, designed,
and photographically re-edited edition of *To the Inland Empire*, published
in clothbound edition in 1987 by Doubleday & Co., Inc.

Designed and typeset in Janson by Deborah Fleig
Maps by Deborah Reade
Manufactured in Korea

10 9 8 7 6 5 4 3 2 1

Library of Congress Cataloging-in-Publication Data
Udall, Stewart L.
    Majestic journey: Coronado's inland empire / by Stewart L. Udall
    photographs by Jerry Jacka
    p. cm.
    Originally published: To the inland empire. Garden City, N.Y. :
Doubleday, 1987.
    Includes index.
    ISBN 0-89013-285-2 (pbk.)
    1. Vázquez de Coronado, Francisco, 1510-1554. 2. America—Discovery
and exploration—Spanish. 3. Southwest, New—Pictorial works. 4. Spaniards—
Southwest, New—History—Pictorial works.
    I. Jacka, Jerry D. II. Title.
    E125.V3U215 1995
    917.604'1'092—dc20   95–281
                                                           CIP

Museum of New Mexico Press
Post Office Box 2087
Santa Fe, New Mexico 87504

Contents

Preface to the
New Edition

THIS BOOK OWES ITS EXISTENCE to Jacqueline Kennedy Onassis. In April 1984, *Arizona Highways* magazine devoted a full issue to a photo article prepared by Jerry Jacka and myself about the *entrada* of Francisco Vázquez de Coronado's 1540 expedition into Arizona. Out of the blue, I mailed a copy of *Highways* to Jackie, then an editor at Doubleday & Co.

The hopeful note I sent along said simply, "Maybe we should collaborate and enlarge this into a book that would tell the whole story?" Her telephone call was positive and enthusiastic, and on learning that she had never seen the Southwest, I invited her to come out and let us introduce her to some of "Coronado's Country."

Jackie liked the idea and in early June she and her companion, Maurice Tempelsman, came west. The week-long Jeep trip Lee and I planned with Jerry and Lois Jacka started in Phoenix and ended in Santa Fe. We went to the Black River crossing, waded the river, and had lunch at that historic site. On the trail down to the White House Ruin in Canyon de Chelly we had to step aside while a Navajo herdsman and his sheep scurried by. Zuni friends showed us the Hawikuh Ruin, and we studied fantastic rock signatures and ruins at El Morro National Monument. We then visited the dramatic Sky City of Acoma, where we viewed the majestic mission church and walked down the stone stairs where the Acoma Indians had once guarded their stronghold.

On trips from Santa Fe we dawdled along the high road to Taos, and, accompanied by Lloyd Kiva New (the *mayordomo* of Indian art) and his wife Azeala, visited a number of Pueblo artists in their homes. And we improvised our own Spanish-history walking tours of Santa Fe, the "City Different."

The handwritten note Jackie sent us when she got home expresses both her personality and her spontaneous reaction to the wonders of the Southwest. Her opening paragraph reads:

☾

*I have never spent such happy days—nor been so absolutely
knocked out by the beauty of all that we saw. It affected
me much more deeply than going to India.
I should have seen America first—but I'm glad I waited
until life gave me the great gift of seeing it all with you.*

☾

Jackie's editorial impact appears on most of the pages of this book. She selected the photographs, sharpened my sentences, and argued with me about the tenor of messages I was trying to convey.

Jacqueline Kennedy Onassis is no longer among us, but we can still enjoy the gifts she gave to the American people. In gladness, and sorrow, we dedicate the new edition of this book to her memory.

STEWART UDALL
SANTA FE, MAY 1995

Preface to First Edition

As the twentieth century wanes, the Coronado epic remains a fascinating subject. It tugs at our minds because missing pieces of evidence continue to tantalize us. The search for facts to enlarge our understanding of this sunrise part of our national story remains an unfinished task for history buffs.

Where, for example, is the exact location of the Chichilticale, the Red House landmark? What parts of the present state of California did that exemplary scout Melchor Díaz traverse when he became the first European afoot in that area? What routes did the expedition follow in what is now West Texas in the summer of 1541? These are only a few of the path mysteries that pique our curiosity.

Two kinds of evidence throw flickers of light on Coronado's wanderings. Most important, of course, are the reports written by participants. These include the overlapping chronicles of Pedro de Castañeda (himself a man of mystery) and Captain Juan Jaramillo. There are the revealing letters Coronado wrote to the viceroy and to King Carlos. There is also testimony presented by Coronado's men at an investigation conducted by a Spanish judge and corroborating facts in a provincial history prepared in 1742 by a Franciscan historian, Mota Padilla.

All of this evidence, and more, was sifted and interpreted by Dr. Herbert E. Bolton when he wrote his authoritative work *Coronado: Knight of Pueblos and Plains*. Bolton was an enthusiast who spent a lifetime enhancing appreciation of our Spanish heritage. He drove and walked across many regions of the U.S. Southwest and Mexico in an effort to match the written stories to the terrain described in the old chronicles. With important exceptions, this book follows Bolton's conclusions. However, Bolton did not check out some leads— and in other instances recent studies have cast doubt on some of his assumptions.

Since Dr. Bolton finished his 1949 Coronado book, for example, a new generation of ethnologists has completed studies that demonstrate that before Columbus there were trade-trail networks connecting the homelands of the inland natives with settlements of their coastal Indian neighbors in northern Mexico.

The location of these networks throws fresh light on Coronado's paths. It explains, for instance, why the conquistadores were never lost and did not waste time hacking trails through wild country. These ancient roads also help explain how the Europeans readily found convenient watering holes or hidden mountain passes.

Where Bolton's conclusions are questioned in this work, a special effort will be made to identify evidence that has come to light since he completed his research.

The small quantity of sixteenth-century Spanish artifacts found thus far in the country Coronado and his men explored is puzzling. This dearth can be explained, in part, by the fact that much of the land they traversed is still a semiwilderness. But even so, it is surprising that few pieces of Coronado hardware—and no actual campsites—have been identified thus far.

Dr. Emil W. Haury, the dean of southwestern archaeologists, believes that "... some of Coronado's weaponry was large enough and durable enough to persist in a dry climate and still attract the probing eye of the twentieth century." To support his thesis, Haury reports that a seventeenth-century Spanish lance he picked up off the ground in 1940 on the Papago Indian Reservation west of Tucson was altered so little by prolonged exposure to the elements that there was still visible the delicate tracery of the Castilian rose motif etched on the face of the blade.

But why have so few of the hundreds of trinkets—made-in-Spain knives, beads, and bells—traded to Indians for food or given away as favors turned up? In the southeastern United States, archaeologists digging in mounds and burial grounds have unearthed dozens of the little brass bells and beads of glass and cut crystal passed out by De Soto and his companions during their 1539–42 *entrada*.

Does the discovery of these De Soto tracers suggest that similar Coronado artifacts will be uncovered as the work of southwestern archaeologists widens? The experts answer this question affirmatively, so there is an inviting prospect that future archaeologists or alert amateurs will uncover Coronado knives or bells or horseshoes or kitchen utensils that, by the quincentennial, in 2040, will link the presence of our conquistadores to precise locations in the American West.

I   Growing up along Coronado's Trail

In My Home Country

IF WE ARE FORTUNATE, mystical echoes that connect our lives to persons and events of other times provide a kind of intermittent background music that adds an element of romance to our existence. The essays in this book represent my effort to share experiences that reverberate back to the European discovery of the land now known as the United States of America—and to a lost century of our history.

An exciting thing happened when I was growing up in a remote area of my native state. This was the revelation that the 1540 expedition of the conquistador Francisco Vázquez de Coronado had passed by my hometown of St. Johns, Arizona, on its quest to find the "golden cities" of Cíbola.

I was six when I went with my father to the crest of the White Mountains to witness the "grand opening" of a dirt road that ran from Alpine down the spine of the Mogollon Rim to the copper town of Clifton. Boosters had prevailed on the state highway department to name this new road the "Coronado Trail," and Arizona's governor was on hand to deliver a dedicatory address.

Flushed with the historical overtones of the occasion, the chief executive recounted Coronado's feats and ended with the peroration: "Who knows, perhaps the axes of Coronado's men rang in these very groves!" At that, a man standing nearby blurted out in a stage whisper, "He doesn't know what he's talking about." I was a rapt listener a few minutes later when he explained to my father that the real trail lay to the west, on the reservation of the Apache Indians, and came by St. Johns as it paralleled the wagon road that later ran from Fort Apache to the Zuni Indian Reservation.

To a child growing up in a lonely land, these revelations were like a fairy tale dropping out of a book into life. Exactly where was the trail? How was it related to such local landmarks as the Black Ridge, the Big Hollow, and the Blue Hills? Were these horsemen who searched for cities of gold carrying flags and banners? Did they camp at our favorite swimming hole at the Meadows? Or stop to fish in the eddies of our little river?

Sometimes when the spring winds were roaring, I would stand and listen. In my imagination I could hear the clang of Spanish armor rising across the hills from the west. And there were daydreams in which I pictured images of multicolored Spanish tents swaying in the breeze. These were the fantasies of my childhood and youth, and they lit a lamp of speculation that flickered on and off as long as I lived in St. Johns.

My second involvement with Coronado's trek came in 1981, after we left Washington, D.C., and came home to Arizona. It started with an innocent memo, to the president of Phoenix's Heard Museum, suggesting that the museum sponsor a three-day educational bus trip to retrace parts of the trail Coronado followed across Arizona. The president, a local judge named Sandra Day O'Connor, sent a crisp response. This concept was a fine idea, and would I be a member of the museum's advisory board and lead such an experimental excursion?

I said yes. Then *Arizona Highways* magazine heard about the trip—and in short order I had also agreed to write a Coronado cover story for that "picturesque" journal. The photographer I teamed up with was another Arizona native, Jerry Jacka, and soon camping trips and frequent excursions to libraries were under way, which generated copy for *Arizona Highways* and led to the decisions that eventually gave birth to this book.

Jerry Jacka is a self-taught photographer who grew up on an Arizona ranch. His love of southwestern landscapes is matched by his interest in Indians and their arts and crafts. Today Jerry stands in the front rank as an interpreter of the western scene. He shares my fascination with the Coronado epic, and most of our camping trips turn into lively discussions of facts we have separately gathered about the land we are traversing.

One of our summer trips to the high country ended in a moment of great excitement after we found a rugged road down to the Black River to a place on a map marked "Government Crossing." Our study of the terrain from the other side of the river had convinced us that this was the only place where horses could have descended the steep gorge of the Black, so our anticipation rose as we studied the matching slopes of two ridges below Big Bonita Creek. We then waded across the river to see if there was a natural path leading up to the Natanes Plateau.

If there was such a trail, I knew this was the old crossing and we had left Jerry's Jeep in a meadow where Coronado had surely pitched a camp. When we found a line of rocks, I remember saying to Jerry, "We are now walking on what is in all probability the oldest identifiable non-Indian historic trail in the United States." It was a moment to savor, for we were now almost certain that Coronado and his men had ridden this trail. And the stacks of rocks told us also that, three hundred and forty years after Coronado's visit, General George Crook had ordered his soldiers to move these rocks and convert the ridge into a military road for packtrains and small wagons.

My imagination had been quickened at many of the national historic sites I had visited, but I felt an extra tug at this place, in my home country. I reminisced how, beginning with Coronado's entrada, horses had played a central role in the unfolding of American history, and I thought that if a time machine could return us to this ridge, we could witness a pageant, spanning six centuries, that would include:

- Indian runners on their way to Mexico in the fourteenth century;

- young Spaniards in the summer of 1540, astride the first European horses ever to stamp the ground in what is now the American West;

- Captain General Coronado leading his downcast army back to Mexico in the spring of 1542;

- Apache Indian warriors, two hundred years later,
  riding off-spring of those Spanish horses to con
  trol this region; and

- in the 1870s, cavalrymen of the U.S. Army on
  maneuvers that would enable them to subdue the
  Apaches and pacify the last Indian-dominated
  area of the United States.

On our next trip, Jerry and I tried to find the site of Coronado's "Camp of Death" on the crest of the White Mountains. After locating what we thought was a logical glen, we drove down the old road to Vernon and climbed one of the cinder knolls on the Springerville road to get a panoramic view of the "land of Cíbola," where Coronado expected to find the seven magical cities. It was a clear day. We could see a hundred miles to the northeast and pick out the silhouette of Towaya' lane, the sacred mountain of the Zuni Indians. Here, too, were all of the vistas—the mesas, buttes, knolls, and natural monuments —I had known and loved in my youth at St. Johns.

As my boyhood curiosities were rekindled in the 1980s, I gradually became a student of the sixteenth century and wondered why we Americans have paid so little attention to the amazing Spanish chapters of our history. And when I looked again at St. Johns, I realized what a unique community it had been in the nineteenth century. My hometown, I saw, was a time window, which could help explain how a primal chapter of our national story got distorted and was almost obliterated.

☾ THE ST. JOHNS TIME WINDOW

On a map, you will find St. Johns south of the Navajo Reservation on the Little Colorado River near the Arizona–New Mexico state line, about forty miles southeast of Petrified Forest National Park. Ancestors of the Pueblo Indians located, and later abandoned, farming communities along this river. (St. Johns polychrome pots found in the area provide an

Arizona: Black River crossing

important date marker for archaeologists.) A second founding came many centuries later, in 1873, when Spanish wagoneers from Santa Fe who were hauling supplies to a new army post at Fort Apache needed a way station and settled a village they named San Juan. These freighters told friends about the lush grasslands they had encountered, and within a short time, Spanish stockmen had driven herds of sheep and cattle across the Continental Divide and were establishing ranches and grazing rights in the region.

In late 1879, a wagon train of Mormon settlers went south from Utah, pitched a camp nearby, and, for the price of five hundred head of cattle, negotiated an agreement to buy a townsite that abutted San Juan on the west. The young bishop who led those colonists was my grandfather, David K. Udall.

In the winter of 1880, he and two cowboys went to Utah, moved a herd of "church cattle" across the frozen Colorado River at Lee's Ferry, and drove them south to complete a land transaction that established a unique cultural confrontation.

A showdown occurred the first day the Mormons began staking out their homesites. A letter of ultimatum delivered to my grandfather advised him that the citizens and public officials of San Juan claimed a "right by antiquity" to expand into the land the Mormons were occupying. (This was an apparent reference to the leave-space-between-settlements arrangements that had worked so well for the Spaniards and the Pueblo Indians in New Mexico.) "Disagreeable consequences" were threatened if the "Mormon sect" did not cease from "surrounding and oppressing" the existing town.

This frontier confrontation, I now realize, occupies an ironic niche in the history of western settlement. It was the only time a band of Brigham Young's faithful fought over a townsite with part of the flock of Archbishop Jean B. Lamy of Santa Fe—and the only instance when my people violated their own leave-space-between-settlements axiom. The Mormons did not want strangers spying on their polygamous way of life, and as long as Brigham Young was alive they intentionally left miles between their colonies and the settlements of disapproving "gentiles."

This coming together is fascinating because both were unpopular minorities. The Mormons were outcasts because of their religious tenets, and the Spaniards were doubly despised by newcomers because of their blood and their religion. Each was a tributary stream running counter to the westward mainstream of development of the United States. St. Johns is an intriguing window to the past because each group of outcasts had stories to tell that refuted legends and "histories" popularized in the East by the white Anglo-Saxon Protestants who were running the country.

Had a foreign journalist (say, a latter-day Alexis de Tocqueville) arrived in New York in 1880 to begin a national tour, the briefings offered by his hosts would have provided a big picture something like this: Since the end of the Civil War, the federal government had concentrated much of its energy on efforts to finish the settlement of the West and make the nation a truly continental country. This plan was proceeding on schedule. Crack units of cavalry were in the final stages of a mop-up campaign to conquer the "savage" Indians, who had been obstructing progress in the West. The army was either removing these hostiles to an Indian territory called Oklahoma or herding them onto Indian reservations, where patrols would keep them permanently pacified. Indians would soon be "swept clean" from entire states such as Texas and Colorado and Kansas. And tens of millions of acres thus wrested from Indian domination were being made available to westbound European immigrants who were filing claims on this free land.

The phrase "the winning of the West" would have been a theme of those briefings. The development of a continental network of railroads—involving lavish grants of national lands to promoters—to weld the nation into a single economic unit would have been another theme. And there would have been predictions that development was moving at such a swift pace, the western frontier would be "closed" in a few years.

Let us suppose that our journalist sensed that this vision of an Anglo-Saxon juggernaut carrying civilization from the East into the wilderness was spinning myths in eastern minds. Let us also assume he perused the latest histories written by Americans and realized that the postwar winning-of-the-West thesis was already a WASP article of faith.

Let us next suppose that our De Tocqueville wanted to go West to study this phenomenon and, by chance, bought a ticket to take him to the end of the railroad under construction in the New Mexico territory—and then rode a horse to St. Johns to conduct interviews with settlers in that community. And finally, we shall pretend that his notebooks were lost and were recently discovered in a family archive in France—and that the following sections were entries in his journal.

☾ THE ST. JOHNS SPANIARDS

An amazing place. Totally surprising. Easterners know nothing about this part of their country. This is a region with its own rich history, one outside the Anglo-Saxon canon.

My hosts are Spaniards. Ancestors here for nearly three centuries. One of their countrymen, Vázquez de Coronado, passed by this village more than 450 years ago and explored from California to Kansas. A second group of Spaniards came in 1598 to Rio Grande Valley, founding a colony years before settlements in Virginia or Massachusetts. These New Mexico settlers were cut off from Spain and Mexico for almost three centuries.

David K. Udall's first home in St. Johns (c. 1880)

They are called Mexicans, for they were part of that country for a few years, but those I have met are Spaniards. Their looks and language tell me this. They speak an old dialect that resembles the Spanish of Cervantes. The years I spent in Madrid studying their history and language gave me many clues about their culture.

They "won" their part of the United States several centuries ago. Eastern emphasis on the 1804–6 Lewis and Clark expedition is strange. Vázquez de Coronado explored the southwest quadrant of the United States 262 years before Jefferson's men explored the northwest.

Spaniards have a different Indian policy. Not savages in their eyes. There was an uprising, but they have lived in peace with Pueblo Indians (and converted some to Catholicism) for two hundred years. Believe removal is brutal mistake. Pueblos live on same land they occupied when Coronado came. A modus vivendi protecting Indian rights was worked out a long time ago.

Astonishing story. Must write about it. But will my eastern friends listen?

St. Johns landscape in the 1890s

☾ The St. Johns Mormons

Sent here from Utah last year. Like the Spaniards, are disciplined, hardworking, attractive people. They defend polygamy; it is a "sacred commandment of the Lord." Hard to identify the polygamy families. Rumor is that some families will soon leave for a haven in Mexico.

Extreme hostility between these two groups. They do not mix. Cultures clash; each religion contends it is the "true church." A strange community. Easterners regard both as pariahs: the Spaniards are a lower class, the Mormons an immoral sect. But in this village each looks down on the other as *the* outcast group. Violence seems inevitable. Tragic, when one considers what they have in common in this lonely country. Wish I could help them understand this.

The Mormons' story also contradicts what I was told in New York. They were driven out of the United States thirty years ago, but soon after they arrived in Utah it was annexed from Mexico. Industrious colonizers. The Mormons have populated Utah and established settlements in six adjoining states and territories. Acting on their own, they have "closed" a huge frontier without any help from the national government. Irony. Anglo-Saxons claim credit for their accomplishments on the frontier even while passing laws to crush their church and put their leaders in prison.

Like Spaniards, Mormons seek amity with Indians. Interviewed Jacob Hamblin, veteran Indian peacemaker for Brigham Young. Impressive man. Regards Indians as equals, speaks their languages. Goes unarmed to settle disputes. Hamblin disagrees with the Indian-removal policy of the national government.

The purpose of this pretending, of course, is to make the point that the eastern WASPs had no interest in insights they could have gained had they paused to view the past from southwestern windows. And our national perspective is still constricted by this blindness: Even in the 1980s, few Americans know about the great pageants and processions that moved across our land in the sixteenth century.

What is personally poignant about the St. Johns story is that all of us acted from a script of intolerance written by others. By missing an opportunity to be true neighbors, we failed to appreciate the rich strands of history our distinctive pioneer cultures represented. In St. Johns, neighborliness had to wait. There were gunfights, vituperative broadsides from rival newspapers, and political trials (one of which sent my grandfather to a federal prison in Detroit) before a standoff came about that resulted in a strange, semisegregated community with separate schools and little social intercourse.

The invisible walls that separated St. Johns were crumbling by the time my generation came along. The worlds of work and sports and politics emphasized our common humanity. But I look back in sadness when I realize that we still wore blinders that deprived us of the opportunity to blend our traditions and share the achievements of our ancestors.

I knew my Hispanic friends, but I did not know their history. I knew that Coronado passed by our town, but I did not grasp that kinsmen of my neighbors might have been soldiers in that magical entrada. I knew that ancestors of these Spaniards had been in the Southwest for a long time, but I did not know that some of my friends were descendants of the first families to found permanent settlements in what is now the United States of America.

A wistfulness evoked by these memories is woven into the fabric of this book.

But this is more than a book about neglected phases of history. The photographs celebrate the land that the first European visitors saw when they entered the Southwest. And they alert us to the interactions between those who came into these uplands and the surrounding environment.

I am enough of a regional chauvinist to believe that Coronado and his companions sensed this region was a place apart. Their march started a process that carved a civilization out of the wilderness they invaded. Some of the country they knew remains unmarred, and the wild, stark beauty they witnessed still lives in those whose senses are attuned to nature's daily benedictions. It is this world of uncommon spaciousness—and the interactions between the truths embodied in its beauty and the human beings who come into its great outdoor galleries—that makes living in the Southwest a spiritual experience.

A source of constant wonder to me is the time-capsule aspect of Coronado's saga: the fact that many of the natural landmarks he and his men saw are still untrammeled. It is astonishing that 80 percent of the land corridor the conquistadores followed from the Arizona border to the outskirts of Albuquerque is, even today, unmarred by cities or surfaced roads.

Although man's imprints deepen as one moves east of the Rio Grande Valley, the photographs offer glorious proof that even in the Great Plains—and on that magnificent mesa that the Spaniards named the Llano Estacado (Staked Plain)—there are a surprising number of unsullied natural areas. Jerry and I began referring to these as Coronadoscapes, and this book contains a sampling of the scenery that Don Francisco and his companions saw as they reconnoitered parts of the greater Southwest. The buffalo and tall grasses are gone from the prairie, but even in West Texas and northeastward into Oklahoma and Kansas, Coronado's path passes small towns and offers occasional glimpses of untrammeled country.

The photographs also remind us that if we look back to antiquity and the Anasazi ancestors of the Pueblo Indians, there has been a timeless interplay of land and people in this part of the world. Geographers have coined words such as scrubland and semiarid to describe parts of the Southwest, but most tend to overlook the drama of survival that has evolved on these tablelands. In lean environments, people are forced to react so intimately with the land that their life patterns, their expectations—and even their religious practices —are shaped by the imperatives of a harsh habitat. I have a vivid memory of one parched weekend in August long ago when the three Colorado Plateau cultures simultaneously beseeched their separate deities to bless the region with rain: the Mormons with a day of fast followed by prayer, the Hopi Indians with their world-famous rattlesnake dance, and the Catholics with processions and special invocations by the padres.

The photographs also hint that adaptation is the key to survival in Coronado's country. The kinds of trees that dominate any natural province indicate the conditions that govern life. Thus, the stunted piñons, junipers, and cedars—whose bushlike branches have dominion in northern Arizona and most of New Mexico—make a powerful statement of dryland adaptation. It is difficult to determine in this region whether people possess the land or the land possesses the people. So it is not surprising that inhabitants of this region exhibit some of the same gnarled, tenacious traits as their trees.

Haniel Long, a poet who lived in Santa Fe, named this region piñon country in his 1941 book of that name. Coronado, I suspect, would have concurred in his thought. When he completed his march through those forests of dwarfed conifers and captured the Zuni village of Hawikuh, he realized that these seemingly useless trees were vital resources for the Indians of Cíbola. One of the succulent stored foods the Zunis offered to Coronado's hungry soldiers was tiny nuts picked from piñon trees. The fuel the Zunis had harvested and stacked alongside their houses to warm their winter days was branches torn from dead trees in those forests. When I contemplate that the same pine nuts and cedar limbs were still important resources four centuries later, during my boyhood days in St. Johns, I see in such continuity an ecological statement of great power.

The photographs that show the spareness of piñon country also reveal the soaring spaciousness and the beauty that must have cast a spell over some of Don Francisco's Spaniards. The chronicles reveal that when the captain general ordered the return to Mexico, in the spring of 1542, sixty soldiers wanted to remain on the Rio Grande and argued that this was "good country" for a colony. In his autobiography, *My Penitente Land*, a direct descendant of the first Spanish colonists, Fray Angélico Chávez, points out how similar New Mexico's landscape is to geographical features of Spain's interior provinces.

This, to me, is one of the most tantalizing episodes of the Coronado epic. After two fruitless years of searching for an elusive Eldorado, what could have persuaded some of those soldiers that this was "good" country? One can understand why the four Franciscan priests, with their yearnings for the garlands of martyrdom, decided to stay. But why, when the comforts of civilization beckoned, did a group of sturdy men want to start a colony from scratch one thousand miles from the nearest outpost of New Spain? What impulses were at work in the minds of those men?

Coronado's decision, in the spring of 1542, to end his quest and start back down the long trail home was a rational one. There were no signs of precious metals or of advanced Indian civilizations. The cold climate was hostile compared to Mexico's lush valleys. And the Pueblo Indians, who had been brutalized, would surely seek revenge if the captain general allowed a party of settlers to remain in the Rio Grande Valley.

The negative factors were so daunting that I am convinced one must consider such intangibles as the well-known Spanish sensitivity to ambience to discover why some of the conquistadores concluded that this was a hospitable environment. Indeed, modern experience supports the surmise that psychological and spiritual values had acquired a grip on the minds of these men. This lean land was "good" because its exceptional natural beauty was uplifting; it was hospitable because its spectacular landscapes offered a promising stage for pioneering; and it was exhilarating because a land mystique hovered over its mesas and mountains and valleys.

Evidence to support this surmise comes from many quarters. D. H. Lawrence came to Taos, marveled at its vistas, and wrote of the "delicate magic" of the culture of the Pueblo Indians. Another artist, Willa Cather, wove the subtle interplay between land and people into her 1927 novel *Death*

Comes for the Archbishop. In addition, the photographs in this book offer pictorial proof of the unusual allure that clings to this enclave.

And there are other witnesses:

The great ecologist Aldo Leopold, who worked as a young forester in Arizona's White Mountains, was awed by the ever-present blue dome of the Escudilla Mountain (which dominates the southern skyline from Zuni). He described this region's "aristocracy of space" and how "life in Arizona was bounded underfoot by grama grass, overhead by sky, and on the horizon by Escudilla."

The naturalist Joseph Wood Krutch looked out from the summit of Navajo Mountain and penned these words:

> *In its own aloof, almost contemptuous, way it is never-*
> *theless extraordinarily beautiful—nature's ultimate*
> *achievement in that Southwestern Style which surprisingly*
> *executes great monolithic forms, sometimes sculptural and*
> *sometimes architectural, in bright multihued sandstone . . .*
> *and in no other [landscape] that I have ever seen is the*
> *pure sensation of space so beautiful or so overwhelming.*

Or listen as the poet/historian Paul Horgan muses over the three communities of Taos:

> *. . . there is a piercing, sweet, illimitable clarity of light*
> *and sky. Sounds carry. Meadowlarks, mockingbirds,*
> *blackbirds have returned. Over the long plain breathes the*
> *wind, sharply sweet and already warmed, disturbing*
> *nothing but the senses. Space is so great, vision is so plain,*
> *air is so clear that human activities can be seen from afar.*

Or read over the shoulder of the young Ansel Adams as he writes to his mentor, Alfred Stieglitz, about his first visit to New Mexico:

*It is all very beautiful and magical here . . . a quality
which cannot be described. The skies and the land are so
enormous and the detail so precise and exquisite that wherever you are, you are isolated in a glowing world between
the macro and the micro—where everything is sidewise
under you and over you, and the clocks stopped long ago.*

It is our good fortune that modern photographers have been able to
capture the magical quality Adams described. There *is* a mystical force that
influences life and living in this part of Coronado's country. I believe that the
ambience it fosters helped sustain the first families who planted a permanent
colony in these United States. It also made it easier for the Spaniards and
Pueblo Indians to make a peace and learn to walk together as friends in this
"good country."

II Those Who Came Before

*The Golden (Spanish) Age
of Discovery: 1492–1542*

*There is no other conquest like this one in the annals of the
human race. In one generation the Spaniards acquired more
new territory than Rome conquered in five centuries.*
—SAMUEL ELIOT MORISON

This was a climactic generation, possibly the *climactic generation in world history, both for what was achieved and for the
future significance of that achievement.*
—J. H. HALE

NOTHING SO EXCITES OUR IMAGINATION as the deeds of those who navi-
gate uncharted oceans, penetrate undiscovered country, and bring back tales
from exotic places. From Odysseus to Marco Polo to Magellan to Edmund
Hillary, explorers have always evoked admiration and wonder.

Although Anglo-Saxon historians have written books about giants of
discovery such as Columbus, Cortés, and Magellan, the reach and splendor
of Spain's golden age of discovery have been slighted. The fantastic surge

across half of the earth by Spain's "climactic generation" has been obscured and ignored.

What was the cause of this neglect? Why, for example, have Anglo historians presented the "age of discovery" as embracing the seventeenth through the nineteenth centuries whereas the paramount work of exploration was done by Spaniards in the first half of the sixteenth century? Why have efforts of the Portuguese and the Spaniards been lumped together, when, by design, one nation explored in the East and the other in the West? Why have we been so slow to concede that in the West the age of discovery belongs to Spain's adventurers?

(PARTITIONING THE PLANET

Both logic and history suggest that the age of discovery should be subdivided into eastern/Portuguese and western/Spanish epochs. Such a delineation conforms to the treaty guideline these nations laid down for their seaborne searches when they fixed the famous line of demarcation 370 leagues west of the Cape Verde Islands and agreed that all to-be-discovered land lying east of it would belong to Portugal, all west to Spain.

The June 1494 Treaty of Tordesillas fascinates us because it was the first, and probably the last, accord between two countries that presumed to partition the planet. Moreover, it was executed at a breathtaking moment when the two most dynamic countries in Europe were poised, like horses at a starting gate, to race into the unknown to define the lineaments of the earth itself.

Windows to the new era were already ajar when diplomats sat down at Tordesillas in the presence of a papal *nuncio* to seal the accord negotiated by the Iberian monarchs. Each country had mariners on the high seas; each nurtured soaring hopes that discoveries were at hand that would bring it unprecedented wealth and power. Six years earlier, Portugal's Bartholomeu Dias had rounded the Cape of Good Hope, and King João, sensing that a sea route to Asia's rich resources was in his grasp, was already preparing the fleet Vasco da Gama would guide all the way to India. Spain's sovereigns were pondering equally auspicious plans, for, just three months earlier, Columbus's messenger Antonio de Torres had ridden the spring tides into Cádiz with the news that the new Admiral of the Ocean Sea was tarrying at the end of his second expedition to establish a Spanish colony on the island of Hispaniola. This development must have persuaded Ferdinand and Isabella that their great captain was laying stepping-stones for a western route to Cathay and the Indies.

The spirit of optimism and cooperation both sides brought to Tordesillas served them well: It gave their treaty a vitality that helped it endure for nearly a century; and it enabled them to avoid conflicts and husband their resources for their separate searches.

In essence, the Treaty of Tordesillas was a friendly wager between "cousins" who were rivals. At the moment the treaty was signed, neither knew there were two worlds, not one, for Europeans to explore and exploit, but each, in effect, was making a private bet with history that its side of the line contained the richest resources. In this instance history was evenhanded, for as the sixteenth century unfolded and vessels bulging with cargoes of spices and precious metals came to anchor in their ports, each country could feel it had made the better bargain.

To understand how Portugal's ingenuity set the stage for these ages of discovery, one must go back a half century to the origins of Portuguese sea power.

☾ PORTUGAL'S EASTERN AGE OF DISCOVERY (1430–1515)

It was an enlightened Portuguese prince, the *infante* Dom Henrique (called by his admirers Prince Henry the Navigator), who started his country on the path to naval supremacy. Dom Henrique had the inquiring mind of a Renaissance man, and his interest in Atlantic seamanship motivated him to set up a center at Sagres, near Cape St. Vincent, to encourage exploration. This was a bold act, for until then pilots had not ventured beyond the comforting confines of the Mediterranean or the near-shore shipping lanes of western Europe and northern Africa.

The *infante* perceived that if Portugal wanted to lead in the Atlantic, innovations were needed. He began his outward-bound program by using part of his royal revenues to promote training exercises that taught his pilots how to use celestial-navigation instruments aboard their ships to fix latitudes and calculate distances. These seagoing experiments—and on-the-job experiences along the African coast—honed Portuguese skills so that by the time of Tordesillas, Portuguese-trained pilots were preeminent, and countries that wanted to undertake long voyages had no choice but to enlist men such as Columbus and Ferdinand Magellan to be the captains of their ships.

Another innovation that enabled Portugal to steal an oceanic march on her continental competitors was the design of a revolutionary new sailing ship, the caravel. The shipwrights who designed these versatile vessels have never been identified, but it is known that the first caravels appeared in Portuguese waters about 1440. Built with two or three masts and rigged with triangular, lateen sails, these ships could tack into the wind and run circles around conventional square-riggers.

By reducing the fearful uncertainty, the addition of these swifter ships made it easier for Prince Henry to coax his mariners westward into the open sea and make longer missions southward along the African littoral. The caravel instilled much confidence, and thus it was no accident that when the time arrived to launch the voyages that changed the world, both Columbus and Bartholomeu Dias chose caravels as the greyhounds of their fleets.

Before he died, in 1460, Dom Henrique's methodical push had produced these landmark discoveries:

- In 1434 Gil Eanes went beyond Cape Nun and returned;
- the nine islands of the Azores Archipelago, 740 miles from the mainland in the Atlantic, were discovered and colonized;
- the Madeira Islands were mapped and settled; and
- by 1460 the Cape Verde Archipelago had been

located, and Prince Henry's pilots had inched
past Dakar and were nearing the equator.

There was a lull after the *infante's* death, but, in the 1470s, King Alfonso V
started an ambitious second wave of exploration with an eye to a trade route
to the Far East. With the aim of finding the southern tip of Africa, Alfonso
gave Fernão Gomes a monopoly on African trade on condition that each
year he would send his pilots at least three hundred leagues farther down the
continent. This big-leap strategy brought ships to the Gold and the Ivory
coasts, and by 1474, Portuguese pilots had crossed the Gulf of Guinea and
established a Portuguese base of operations on the island of Fernando Po.

Alfonso's successor, João II, was equally aggressive. In 1481, this monarch
outfitted a royal fleet of eleven ships to build a huge fort on the Gold Coast.
This exercise had happy consequences for both Portugal and Spain, for one
of the sharp-eyed sailors who trained on this trip was a native of Genoa,
Christopher Columbus.

João, the smell of eastern spices in his nostrils, was quick to capitalize on
his gains: by 1464, Diogo Cão had reached the mouth of the Congo River,
and only four years later, three caravels under the command of Dias went
around a cape his king soon named Good Hope and swept northward until
a mutinous crew forced him to trim his sails and head home.

No one has ever explained why Portugal's rulers waited nine years after
Dias returned with his electrifying news before they sent out a follow-up
fleet, but there is ample proof they were confident a seaway to India and the
Spice Islands was within their grasp. This knowledge can be deduced from
the circumstance that when Manoel I was installed as monarch, in 1495, he
had himself proclaimed ". . . lord of the conquest, navigation, and commerce
of India, Ethiopia, Arabia, and Persia."

The mariner picked by Manoel to fulfill this destiny was Vasco da Gama.
Da Gama left Lisbon with four ships in 1497. He followed the sea path pioneered by Dias around the great cape, methodically worked his way up the
eastern coast of Africa to Mombasa, and finally set sail for Calicut. When he
learned there were Arabian pilots who knew the winds and ways of the Indian

Ocean, with typical Portuguese caution he commandeered their services and had them guide him on his twenty-three-day run to the Malabar Coast.

Da Gama's triumphal return, in 1499, was a signal to Manoel that he should marshal his resources and establish hegemony over the whole region before the Spaniards found a backdoor cape or strait of their own and began building bases in Eastern waters. With unaccustomed speed, the young king got a second expedition, led by Pedro Alvares Cabral, on the high seas. He organized and orchestrated his national effort with such verve that within fifteen short years his nation was master of a vast trading empire that stretched from Socotra, at the entrance to the Red Sea, to Ormuz, at the mouth of the Persian Gulf, to Malacca, to China—and on to the fabled Spice Islands.

It was at this juncture that the prowess and discipline nurtured since the days of Prince Henry gave Portugal the sailors, naval captains, and technical skills it needed to sweep the Moslem naval forces from the Indian Ocean and seize strongpoints ashore to command the avenues of inland trade. Among the great captains who gave Portugal the first global empire were the following:

- Cabral, who in a single voyage that began in 1500 became the codiscoverer of the bulge of Brazil, the explorer who first put the island of Madagascar on the map, and the founder of a trading depot at Cochin, south of Calicut;

- Da Gama himself, at the head of an armed fleet of fourteen ships, who defeated a navy assembled by the Malabar Arabs and forced concessions that made Kilwa (in Zanzibar) a permanent bastion for his country; and

- Almeida, the first viceroy sent east by the king, who demonstrated the superiority of Portuguese firepower off Diu in 1509 when he crushed a combined Gujarati and Egyptian fleet.

However, it was the next viceroy, the master strategist and administrator Alfonso de Albuquerque, who put in place a system of commercial and naval fortresses in the Middle East that wiped out the remnants of the Arab spice trade. Albuquerque perceived that Portugal had to station a powerful, permanent naval patrol in the Indian Ocean to protect its trade routes, and by 1514 the brilliant execution of his strategic plan had given Portugal control over Oriental commerce. A daring gambler who always won his wagers, with a series of quick strokes Albuquerque, by 1515, had consummated the Eastern age of discovery by sending successful exploring expeditions to the Chinese city of Canton and to new pickup ports in the Spice Islands.

This magnificent achievement was, of course, made possible by teamwork and discipline and by the extraordinary sea skills the Portuguese had perfected. These Portuguese were intrepid, but the most remarkable thing about Portugal's Eastern age of discovery was that it was carried out by a tiny nation of only two million people!

Portugal stood by itself on a global promontory in 1515—only to see its great accomplishments swiftly excelled in three short decades by its Iberian brothers.

☾ THE SPANISH PAGEANT OF EXPLORATION

Spain was not landbound during the period when Prince Henry and those he tutored were engaged in pioneering in the Atlantic. She had regular traffic with her colonies in the Canary Islands; and after Queen Isabella pushed her Castilian mariners to compete in the African trade, a naval showdown occurred, in 1478, in which Portuguese captains used superior ships and sailing skills to smash a Spanish flotilla of thirty-five ships.

It is ironic that the great pathfinding voyage of Christopher Columbus, which opened the door to Spain's own age of discovery, was an outgrowth of the 1478 disaster. The victorious Alfonso successfully insisted that there be a treaty declaring the African coast out of bounds for Spanish seamen. This meant that if Ferdinand and Isabella wanted to entertain dreams of an overseas empire, they had to turn their eyes westward to the uncharted seas beyond the Azores.

We do not know how Columbus reached his conclusion that ships could sail west and reach China and the spiceries of the East. We do know, however, that by 1483, after he had studied the techniques of Portuguese mariners, his "enterprise of the Indies" concept was full-blown and he was making the rounds trying to persuade one of Europe's kings that the time had come to discover the East by sailing west across the Atlantic.

The event that apparently opened one royal mind to the potential of Columbus's plan was the overthrow, in the early months of 1492, of the Moorish stronghold of Granada, the last redoubt of Muslim power on the Spanish mainland. This triumph put an ebullient Queen Isabella in a frame of mind to impulsively approve the gamble that launched what Samuel Eliot Morison would later describe as "the greatest recorded voyage in history."

This essay is not the place to dwell on the details of Columbus's initial odyssey. The work of Christopher Columbus is important because his deeds provided a springboard for those who followed. Columbus encouraged Spaniards to nurture wild dreams: What made his influence endure was his persistence—and his willingness to write his own script when he encountered obstacles at the edge of the known world.

In a little more than two decades after his first landfall, he and his followers had

- Mapped the islands of the Antilles;
- explored the rim of the Caribbean in a strenuous search for a west-running strait;
- discovered the Florida Peninsula;
- hacked through the Isthmus of Panama to view the Pacific; and
- traveled along the coast of Brazil southward as far as the Plata River.

These feats laid the groundwork for the great surge that would carry his countrymen to their breathtaking climax in 1542. The permanent colonies

Columbus planted—with their horse farms and shipwrights and blacksmiths —meant that Spaniards came to stay and would be equipped to plunge inland or to follow the call of far-off places. The land sailors who later called themselves conquistadores did not exist when Columbus died, in 1506, but it was the great admiral who set the example they later followed when he led an expedition into the hinterland of Hispaniola. Spain, in the end, would excel Portugal because she dared to explore the inland regions of the continents she discovered.

In a sense, the real greatness of Christopher Columbus lay in the fact that he was an incomparable teacher/drillmaster for his adopted country: He taught that there are times when life itself must be put at risk; he demonstrated that in new environments one had to improvise and to be indefatigable; he showed that exploring the land could be as important as sailing new seas; and he also taught that the quest for a strategic strait was more important than an ephemeral search for gold.

It is not an overstatement to say that, once Columbus finished his work in the New World, the explosive outcome of Spanish exploration was foreseeable. Figuratively, all of the superb Spanish captains of the sixteenth century were Columbus's children. Even Cortés, as he faced the mountains of Mexico and dismantled his boats on the beaches of Vera Cruz, was—as he stretched self-reliance to the point of insubordination—a symbolic child of the Admiral of the Ocean Sea. This man from Genoa built a huge bonfire on a hill, and the men who came after him lit their ambitions from its embers.

☾ CORTÉS

He was a man from Medellín, in the province of Estremadura, who found glory in the New World. We automatically link his name to the conquest of Mexico, to Montezuma, to the golden ornaments of the Aztec Empire. But he was more than the first of Spain's conquistadores: Hernán Cortés was pivotal because he provided a drive-inland impetus that, in two swift decades, gave the Spanish dominion over the most spacious empire ever created on earth.

Cortés was trained in law, not military science, and those who have studied his life have been intrigued by the power of his imagination and the elegance of his mind. He was a conqueror who could lead armies; but he was also, a companion noted, "something of a poet." He had enormous energy and knew how to use force efficiently, but one of his greatest gifts was an intuition that informed him when *not* to use force, when it was better to apply guile or kindness or flattery. Cortés's greatness as a conquistador was part of his larger greatness as a diplomat, for his real genius came from insights that allowed him to manage events (and not let them manage him), to understand the intricacies of Indian psychology, and to evoke a loyalty in his men that manifested itself in rare forms of bravery.

In reality, Hernán Cortés (not King Carlos) was the geopolitician who galvanized a wave of inland exploration that fixed the continental metes and bounds of the Spanish Empire in two short decades. Cortés did more than subdue the Aztecs and seize their gold: He demonstrated that, on a frontier, diplomacy could be more important than military force and that alliances with natives could provide the manpower needed to overcome massive armies.

It is true, of course, that the prizes Cortés captured from the Aztecs added an aura of gold fever to the conquistador concept. After the conquest of Mexico, most of the conquistadores were driven by the hope that other "gilded lands" (Eldorados) would be discovered. But beyond the lure of metallic bonanzas, what encouraged conquistadores to undertake "impossible" expeditions was the Cortesian lesson that the number of soldiers a leader had under his command was not important if he respected Indian needs and understood Indian psychology.

It took time for aspiring conquistadores to get commissions from Seville and organize their expeditions, but by 1535 a tidal wave of inland exploration was under way in South America:

- An expedition under Pedro de Mendoza was on its way to found the city of Buenos Aires;
- Diego de Almagro was ready to begin the conquest of Chile;

- the Inca Empire had been overpowered by Cortesian tactics, and another, more ruthless Estremaduran, Francisco Pizarro, was building a capital for Peru at Lima;

- the city of Quito had been established by Belalcázar;

- the conquest of Colombia was under way, and Bogotá would shortly be founded by Quesada;

- several successful colonies had been planted in Venezuela; and

- the exploration of Mexico had reached as far north as Culiacán, in the present Mexican state of Sinaloa.

Cortés, who had fired the salvo that launched this vast effort, was still in Mexico in 1535 nursing false hopes that the king would approve his plans for northern entradas to explore the area of the "northern mystery." A new viceroy would make the decisions that sent Francisco Vázquez de Coronado and other, younger men to carry out these conquests. But, as we shall soon see, the old lion would live to witness, in 1542, a culmination that would bring Spanish outreach to an apex he could not have envisioned when he led his men onto the beaches at Vera Cruz in 1519.

☾ MAGELLAN

Of the three greatest navigators in the age of discovery—Columbus, Magellan, and Vasco da Gama— Magellan stands supreme. . . . [His] was the greatest and most wonderful voyage in recorded history.
—SAMUEL ELIOT MORISON
The Great Explorers

Had the rulers of sixteenth-century Spain done nothing but sponsor the first odyssey of circumnavigation, they would have secured a preferred place for their nation in the pantheon of discovery. Let us backtrack to 1519 and follow the developments that brought this remarkable enterprise to fruition.

Born to a noble family and once a page to the queen, Ferdinand Magellan spent most of his life as a Portuguese patriot. He went to the Far East as a volunteer with Almeida's armada in 1505, stayed for six years, participated in the great naval battle of Diu, was wounded in a skirmish at Malacca, commanded a caravel on a reconnaissance of the Spice Islands of Ambon and Banda (which supports the thesis he was the first person to encircle the earth), and later survived a shipwreck in the Maldive Islands.

One can deduce that, by the time he returned home, Ferdinand Magellan was nursing Columbus's old hunch that there was a shortcut passage to the Far East through a strait hidden in the southern continent of the New World. However, when he was repeatedly rebuffed by a king who was too busy counting his nation's gains from its burgeoning eastern empire to be interested in investing in hunches, Magellan took a cue from Columbus, went to Seville, became a Spanish subject, and doggedly set out to sell his plan to the sovereign of his new country.

It was now 1518, and Magellan found a warmer reception when he gained an audience with King Carlos at his palace in Valladolid. Carlos, an ambitious young monarch, was undoubtedly envious of Portugal's monopoly of the lucrative spice trade—and we can also surmise that he was fascinated that a Portuguese defector who had navigated in the Far East was convinced that the riches of the Spice Islands lay on the Spanish side of the line of demarcation. It was an auspicious hour, both for Magellan and the inhabitants of the planet, when the young king endorsed the bold mission proposed by this stranger.

Through the fidelity of Spain's archivists, we have an eyewitness account of Magellan's encounter with King Carlos. Bishop Bartolomé de Las Casas (whom we shall meet later as the great champion of the Indians of the Americas) was present and wrote that Magellan ". . . brought with him a well-painted globe showing the entire world, and thereon traced the course he proposed to take, save that the strait was purposely left blank so no one could anticipate him." Later on, the bishop also observed that the Portuguese mariner ". . . must have been a brave man . . . although his person did not carry much authority, since he was of small stature and did not look like much."

The good bishop was not the only one misled by Magellan's physique. Terror was an invisible passenger on Magellan's frail ships, and intimations of mutinous behavior—attitudes that would culminate in a full-blown rebellion against "Portuguese leadership" in the icy waters of Patagonia—were in evidence soon after the expedition became seaborne. Magellan was outnumbered, but inner steel made him the master, and he quelled mutinies and kept his ships on course. Poured from the same mold as Christopher Columbus, he did not question his own assumptions, and his expectant eyes were always on the horizons of the west. Ferdinand Magellan's mettle was tested every day of the last voyage of his life, and he passed every test until he made the misjudgment on Mactan Island that cost him his life.

The grim and glorious odyssey of Magellan and his ships is well known. The efforts of Portuguese agents to abort his mission, the agonizing stop to winter over in the near-arctic air of Patagonia, the mutinies and the "lost" ship that turned back to Spain, the fearsome beauty of the "strait which bears his name," the immensity of the great ocean beyond the strait, the ox hides and rats eaten by starving, scurvy-ridden men on the long voyage to Guam, and the 115 sailors out of the 150 who came through the strait but did not live to return home are familiar facts to students of this saga of circumnavigation. Familiar too is the story of the naval finesse demonstrated by Magellan's successor, Sebastián Elcano, who brought the *Victoria* and her emaciated crew directly across the Indian Ocean, around the Cape of Good Hope, and back to an anchorage in Seville.

The *Victoria* carried a rich load of spices, but it was her other cargo—the geographical knowledge gathered on her three-year odyssey—that had incalculable value for mankind. In the will he dictated before he boarded his flagship, Magellan modestly wrote that he was "bound for the Moluccas." He was modest to a fault, for the journey he launched became the most significant scientific expedition of all time.

The voyage of the *Victoria* is imperishable because it announced with finality that the world was round and could be rounded. It also gave Europe's geographers authentic measurements about the earth's largest ocean and its relationship to the landmass of Asia. And it brought seminal facts for geographers and mariners about the sizes and shapes of continents and archipelagos.

The gift Spain and her intrepid sailors offered to mankind in 1522 was a radiant sphere: an outline of a whole earth with signposts to Edens yet to be discovered. It was a message that has reverberated down the centuries, for this voyage dispelled ancient apprehensions about the unknown and irrevocably altered the potential for human endeavor on the planet.

☾ THE INCOMPARABLE CLIMAX OF 1542

In all the annals of exploration, there is no year that has the luster of 1542. No one in Seville planned it that way, but 1542 was the great climax of the Spanish age of discovery—a year in which Spain had expeditions under way that stretched halfway around the globe in a vast circle from California to Kansas to North Carolina to the Amazon River to the pampas of southern Brazil to Chile's Atacama Desert to Luzon, in the newly named Philippine Islands, and back across the Pacific to the shores of Oregon.

Three centuries would elapse before all of the earth's unknown places were identified and explored—but never again would any nation even contemplate the incredible outreach achieved by Spain's sea captains and conquistadores from 1539 to the culmination of 1542. This Spanish flood tide crested in 1542; there would be a few significant discoveries later—and the sun after 1542 would always shine on colonies of Spanish settlers—but the great days were done when the new year arrived in 1543.

One must unroll maps of the Pacific and the entire Western Hemisphere to trace the travels of these second-wave explorers. As Spanish exploration climaxed exactly fifty years after Columbus's first voyage, all of these expeditions were in the field or on the high seas:

- The first journey across what is today the southern sector of the United States was completed in 1542 when Hernando de Soto was buried in the great river he had discovered after a three-year trek that took him and his men across parts of Florida, Georgia, and North Carolina to the headwaters of the Tennessee River and then on a reconnoiter southward to the Mobile area and over sections of Alabama and Mississippi and beyond into western Arkansas;

- Francisco Vázquez de Coronado and his captains (whose footsteps we shall follow) returned to New Spain in the spring of 1542 after a two-year epic that made them the first Europeans to set foot in California, to see the Grand Canyon, to live among the Pueblo Indians, and to explore the Great Plains on the way to the homeland of the Quivira Indians, in central Kansas;

- the same year, Juan Rodríguez Cabrillo left the port of Navidad and sailed up the Baja California coast to discover San Diego Bay and the Channel Islands of California; Cabrillo died, but not before ordering his mate, Ferrelo, to venture on up the California coast, where he and his shipmates made the first sighting of what is now Oregon in 1543; and

- it was Ruy López de Villalobos, sailing from Navidad the same year, who pioneered a mid-Pacific route to the archipelago he named the Philippines (in honor of the crown prince, Felipe) on a voyage that laid down nautical signposts for later expeditions by Legazpi and Friar

Urdaneta, which paved the way for Spain's
"Route of the Manila Galleon" monopoly of
transpacific shipping for 250 years.

The Southern Hemisphere witnessed similar culminations in 1542.
Among the milestones were the following:

- The completion of the two-year float trip down
  the Amazon River by Francisco de Orellana,
  who had climbed the snowy spine of the
  Peruvian Andes to the headwaters of the world's
  largest river;

- the arrival at Asunción of the walking party that
  had been led on a thousand-mile trek across the
  savannas of southern Brazil by Alvar Núñez
  Cabeza de Vaca, who left his name on the other
  American continent with a similarly stupendous
  trek; and

- the consummation of the final, fruitless search
  for a midcontinent waterway to the Pacific up
  the estuary of the Paraguay River by Domingo
  Martínez de Irala.

Taken together, these sorties and entradas constitute a Himalayan moment
for geography. Never again would any country have a year—or even a century!
—when its explorers would range so far or add so much to the store of knowledge about earth's unknown places. One must telescope two centuries of
history—pretend, for instance, that the latter-day quests of Captain Cook,
Vitus Bering, Lewis and Clark, Luis Vaez de Torres, and David Livingstone
were the work of a single nation in a single year—to amass a list that can be
compared with the achievements of Spain's "class of 1542."

But why, you ask, has this astonishing climax never been put into focus
and recognized in North America? There are three interrelated answers: The

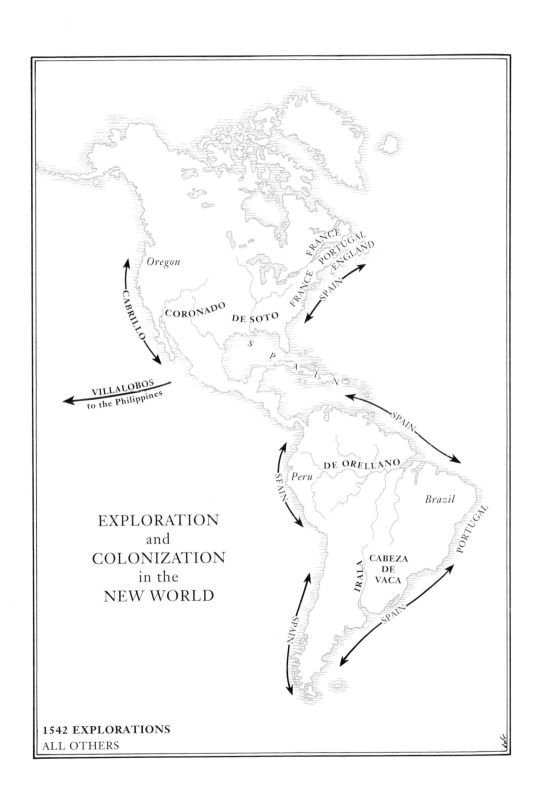

Oregon

CABRILLO

CORONADO   DE SOTO

FRANCE
FRANCE PORTUGAL
ENGLAND
FRANCE
SPAIN

S P A I N

VILLALOBOS
to the Philippines

SPAIN

DE ORELLANO

SPAIN
Peru

Brazil

EXPLORATION
and
COLONIZATION
in the
NEW WORLD

IRALA   CABEZA
DE
VACA

PORTUGAL

SPAIN

SPAIN

1542 EXPLORATIONS
ALL OTHERS

first reminds us of the anti-Spanish blinders worn for so long by many students of history; the second suggests that so much time has been spent extolling the feats of Spain's great triumvirate (Columbus, Magellan, and Cortés) that there was little energy left to concentrate on the deeds of the second-wave explorers; and the third is that so many freelancers were in the field—so many expeditions were under way—that not even the king's men in Seville were fully aware of the surge that brought Spain's age of discovery to this culmination.

An epoch crested in 1542: The conquistadores, their missions accomplished, faded away; future sea captains used their skills principally to secure the sea-lanes of Spain's new empire; and the new generation of leaders sent to the West were administrators, who made governments function and who presided over the erection of cities, churches, and universities. A new kind of explorer, the mineral locator, appeared in the 1540s: the new favorites of the crown were the mining men who, in 1545, uncovered rich outcroppings of silver ore at Potosí, in Bolivia, and Zacatecas, in Mexico. It was these and later discoveries that gave Spain a new source of wealth that dwarfed the value of the ornaments and golden gewgaws seized earlier from the Aztecs and the Incas.

For Spain, three events signaled the close of its age of discovery and the initiation of a new era of consolidation. These were the creation of European universities in Mexico and Peru in the 1550s, the king's edict in 1551 that forbade further expeditions of conquest, and the 1566 voyage of Legazpi and Urdaneta ordered by King Felipe himself with the goal of establishing a new kingdom in Manila and finding a sea route for regular commerce between the Far East and New Spain.

☾ Was It a Spanish Age?

Within three generations Spaniards discovered, subdued, and colonized the most extensive territorial empire the world had ever seen, performed prodigies of valor and endurance, and created a civi-

*lized and sophisticated society in the midst of a virgin
wilderness.*

—CLARENCE HARING,
HISTORIAN, HARVARD UNIVERSITY

The evidence is indisputable that Spanish, not "European,"
explorations were predominant in the West in the fifty-year period that followed
the landfall of Columbus. Having examined the reach of Spanish conquests,
let us compare the efforts of her supposed rivals during this same period.

England achieved the least in the New World from 1492 to 1542. Her
only ventures took English seamen on short trips along the coasts of Labrador
and Newfoundland—and the claim that her most famous explorer of this
period, John Cabot, established some kind of "title" to North America by two
voyages to its eastern edge in 1497 and 1498 is a transparent fiction. As events
demonstrated time after time in the century that followed, effective dominion
in the New World was asserted only when a nation planted colonies and provided logistical and naval support that enabled settlers to carve out claims
other countries had to respect.

France, a late starter, held off commencing systematic exploration in the
West until after Verrazano had reconnoitered part of the eastern coasts of
the United States and Canada in 1524. It took the news of the combined discoveries of Columbus, Cortés, and Magellan to stir the French rulers from
their torpor. True, France sent the redoubtable Jacques Cartier in the 1530s
to explore the St. Lawrence River and its land corridor. But despite his efforts
to build a base for future settlements, in 1542 France had no real foothold in
North America.

Portugal achieved more, but her western accomplishments were, of
course, circumscribed by her adherence to the line of demarcation. Portugal
was the only European power that had permanent western colonies by 1542.
These settlements came about when Pedro Alvares Cabral unexpectedly
sighted a mountain on the bulge of Brazil while on a "great circle" route to
India in 1500 to secure the beachhead established by Vasco da Gama. Cabral's
compass told him this landmass (explored in greater detail the same year by

the Spaniard Vicente Yáñez Pinzón) was on Portugal's side of "the line"—
and in due course King Manoel notified his Spanish cousin that the area was
subject to his sovereignty. Portugal waited thirty years to tie down this claim,
but by 1542 she had a few struggling settlements along the Brazilian coast.

The aggressive Portuguese also encouraged their fishermen/mariners to
explore the North Atlantic. In 1501–2, Gaspar Corte-Real probably coasted
sections of Newfoundland for the first time. Thirty years later, his countryman
João Ivares Fagundes discovered the Bay of Fundy and set up a short-lived
fishing village on Cape Breton Island. However, Portugal did not carve out a
base in North America and later funneled her colonizing energies into Brazil.

(The Spanish Achievement

Comparison with Portugal not only accentuates the reach
and the dynamism of Spanish exploration, it also dramatizes the extent to which
Spain's accomplishments in the first half of the sixteenth century dwarfed
those of her neighbors. If one surveys the immense stage of the Western
Hemisphere and measures achievement by new continents discovered, new
sailing routes pioneered, miles of coastline investigated, or acres of the surface
of the earth traversed, it is clear that the explorers of other European countries were bit players during the entire drama of the Spanish age of discovery.

In every category, Spain's hegemony was overwhelming. Spain had a dozen
sea captains who individually sailed farther and saw more new landscapes in
the West than John Cabot and Verrazano and Cartier and Cabral combined.
Spain was the only country whose explorers organized inland entradas and
carried out conquests on horseback, on rafts, and on foot ranging for thousands of miles across the Americas. The Spanish mariners who measured the
girth of the Pacific and studied its winds, islands, and archipelagoes had that
great ocean all to themselves for the first eighty-seven years of the sixteenth
century. Only Spain had a Magellan, a Cortés, a Coronado. Spain, in short,
created an empire on land and on the seas while her European rivals were
studying shorelines from their ships.

This was a prescient moment for the human race. The winds that billowed the sails of incoming ships also billowed the potential of life itself. The idea that evolved into "the American dream" was incubated by the Spanish age of discovery. It was no accident that in the year 1516 Sir Thomas More's *Utopia* was published or that in the following year the philosopher Erasmus wrote these words in his diary:

> *Immortal God, what a world I see dawning.*
> *Why can't I grow young again?*

The feats of Spain's golden hour were awesome. This small planet held only one Pacific Ocean and one new hemisphere. After 1542 it would not be possible for any country to match the outreach achieved by Spain—or for any explorers to excel the accomplishments of her discoverers.

The Indian Hosts

> *However, Zuni religion is not limited to special times or places.*
> *It encompasses life every day, anywhere. . . . The Zuni believe*
> *that everyone carries within himself his own personal "life road."*
> —EDMUND J. LADD,
> ANTHROPOLOGIST,
> MEMBER OF THE ZUNI TRIBE

> *It was an organized life whose ruling ideas were order, modera-*
> *tion, unanimity. . . . But the Pueblo people had no ruler. . . . The*
> *irresistible power which ordered their lives was the combined*
> *and voluntary power of the people."*
> —PAUL HORGAN
> *The Heroic Triad*

Between november 1519, when Hernán Cortés started inland from the beaches of Vera Cruz, and 1542, when the De Soto and Coronado expeditions began retreating to Mexico, Spanish conquistadores in pursuit of Eldorados conducted what amounted to an informal inventory of the aboriginal cultures of the New World. This "survey" reached from central Chile to a far-off rim in the north that stretched from North Carolina to Kansas to New Mexico.

When this great burst of exploration was completed, these Spaniards concluded that they had discovered two impressive indigenous civilizations and a wide range of other Indian groups in various stages of development. The two supposedly highest cultures—the Aztec and the Inca—belonged to natives whose rulers could be compared with Europe's royal houses. They controlled far-flung "empires" through the use of military force and were adept at gathering nuggets of gold and casting them into handsome ornaments.

This assessment of the Aztec and the Inca remained the verdict of history until our century, when anthropologists cast doubts on earlier conclusions and developed new criteria for assessing the contributions of particular cultures. Not only has the value of such things as precious metals and evanescent military feats been downgraded but some have insisted on weighing such supposed intangibles as religion, social organization, and moral leadership in the scales against technical and martial achievements. The poet T. S. Eliot once asserted that authentic culture is "the incarnation of the religion of a people."

Modern critics have questioned the esteem formerly accorded societies for producing egotistical public works that served no redeeming community purpose—and expressed puzzlement about the admiration once accorded short-lived empires forged by the vainglorious campaigns of charismatic military leaders. In an epoch when sustainability must be a cardinal goal for mankind, it has been argued that we should value cultures that have persisted because people understood the importance of stability and learned how to curb their aggressive instincts and those of their neighbors.

Does not long-term survival over many centuries by such cultures as the Jews of the Diaspora and the Pueblo Indians of the southwestern United States exemplify a philosophy that may be indispensable if mankind is to avert a nuclear ecocatastrophe?

That longevity should be a hallmark of a superior civilization throws new light on the indigenous cultures of the New World. It also raises questions about the Aztecs and the Incas and puts the two-year visit that Francisco Vázquez de Coronado made to the homeland of the Pueblo Indians more than 450 years ago in a different perspective.

The Aztecs and the Incas

Although they lived unknown to each other on different continents—the Aztecs in what is now Mexico, the Incas in South America—there were many striking similarities between their cultures before the Spaniards arrived in the New World. Both enjoyed fertile soil and had learned specialized techniques of irrigation and the cultivation of nutrient-rich terraces that enabled them to achieve breakthroughs in agricultural output. Both had created imposing urban centers as capitals by using architectural skills to construct impressive temples and public works. Each had craftsmen who were excellent weavers and potters. And each lived where a profligate nature had strewn random nuggets of gold across the landscape and had responded by inventing methods of gathering this precious metal and casting it into objects of art.

The rise to power of these two minor tribes began a bare century before the conquistadores appeared. If one attributes the beginnings of Inca power to the leadership of Pachacutec, the year 1438 is a landmark in Inca history; and if the consolidation of Aztec domination is ascribed to Moctezuma I, 1440 is a comparable milestone for the Aztec Indians.

But there were differences as well as similarities. If Inca culture deserves to be ranked as more advanced than that of the Aztecs, it is because its founders combined soldierly prowess with talents for social organization and civic planning. Sir Clements Markham called Pachacutec "the greatest man that the aboriginal race of America has produced." In a hectic half century of expansion, he and his son, Tupac, extended family control over a vast region in the Andes, from Ecuador to central Chile, which encompassed a population of perhaps ten million people.

Pachacutec and Tupac were exceptional because they were apparently as interested in colonization as in plunder, being more intent on establishing patterns of peaceful commerce than on changing the cultures of the groups they had subdued. There is evidence that by combining strict discipline with measures that provided some modest benefits to their new subjects, the Incas, after their wars were won, did constructive things. They used some of their energies to build vast highways and a trading system that improved the lot of the entire empire.

In the end, however, it was a civil war and the regimentation of this centralized Inca apparatus—its emphasis on robotlike obedience to orders from above—that betrayed the Inca rulers. It allowed Francisco Pizarro and his tiny band of Spaniards to seize the reins of Inca power with very little force. When Pizarro executed King Atahualpa and began issuing orders in his stead, to his amazement the wheels of the docile Inca bureaucracy turned with the same efficiency as before.

Although this bureaucracy—and the gold gathered by the minions of the "emperor"—was supposedly the main emblem of Inca greatness, its one durable contribution to the human race came from a more down-to-earth achievement. It was the anonymous Andean farmers, who nurtured varieties of potatoes, squash, tomatoes, peanuts, manioc, and chili peppers (none of which grew in the Old World!), who made a lasting contribution to the world food supply. The potato is today the most important vegetable in the world; it, along with Indian maize and peanuts, now provides more than 40 percent, by weight, of the total food consumed by inhabitants of this planet. Truly, this was the "golden" gift of New World natives to humanity.

Many of the manifestations of higher civilization developed by the Aztecs were comparable to Inca accomplishments. Apparently, few of the Aztec warrior kings were organizers, but the second Moctezuma—who came to power in 1502 and governed when Cortés came to his capital of Tenochtitlán—had in two decades created a hugh administrative superstructure that included governors of provinces, tax collectors, courts, official messengers, and military garrisons. His system has been described as an "Oriental-type political organization," for Moctezuma was a despot surrounded by a powerful caste of priests who presided over the ongoing deification of his person.

In addition to high yields achieved by irrigation and by the "floating garden" agriculture of the Aztecs, as well as trade and tax policies that funneled wealth into the Valley of Mexico, the engineering project that most impressed the Spaniards was a large waterway. Plied by as many as two hundred thousand

Arizona: Petroglyphs along the White River near Canyon Day

boats, it connected a system of lakes through artificial canals and enabled the Aztecs to concentrate a dense population and vigorous commerce in the central part of the land area they dominated.

Yet, despite their conquests, their "brilliant" bureaucracies, their advances in agriculture, and their impressive public works, the abrupt collapse of the Aztec and Inca empires raises perplexing questions. Why, for example, did the Aztec and the Inca people exhibit so little loyalty to their rulers, their rituals, and their deities? Why did the sinews of religious belief that presumably held these societies together melt away like sand castles on a seashore when the first wave of European culture washed ashore in the New World? What, indeed, were the shortcomings that made these societies so brittle, so short-lived?

New Mexico: Petroglyph of Avanu (water serpent) in the Galisteo Basin

Each, of course, had the inherent strengths and defects of any theocratic government that lodges all power in a living "god" surrounded by a small circle of relatives and powerful priests who interpret and carry out his commands. Under such "divine" dictatorships, there was no sharing of power, there was a truncated sense of community, and there was no room for goals or life plans for individuals.

There is ample evidence that the scheme of worship that evolved under the Aztec rulers was primarily a religion for the extended royal family, not for ordinary Aztecs. Its cult of personality, its reliance on the loyalty of "citizens" who had only a small stake in its success, and its debilitating policy of continuous war to capture prisoners for the daily sacrificial ceremonies of its priests made it as vulnerable to winds of change as a great tree with a tiny taproot on a windswept hill.

It was the savage core of the Aztec creed that ensured that the duration of its empire would be brief. The cult of sacrifice demanded a daily flow of human blood from altars that were the butcher shops of priests. This was the

mortal flaw of the Aztec religion. It inculcated terror wherever the Aztecs had
dominion. It eliminated the kinds of peaceful partnerships with conquered
peoples that the Incas effectuated in parts of their empire. This policy of slow
genocide stiffened the resistance of powerful nations like the neighboring
Tlaxcalans and made them irreconcilable enemies of Tenochtitlán.

Cortés had the genius to
feel the pulse of events as he
worked his way into the
Valley of Mexico. He sensed
that Aztec power might self-
destruct if he used the right
mixture of diplomacy and
force. And once he realized
that the natives of Tlaxcala
were implacable foes of the
Aztecs, he made the war
alliance that sealed the doom
of the latter's civilization.

Similarly, although Inca
rule was more humane and
its subject peoples were
treated with greater respect,
once Pizarro seized
Atahualpa, his empire fell
under Spanish control within
a few weeks. Some of the

*New Mexico: El Morro National Monument. Spanish
inscriptions alongside ancient Indian petroglyphs*

same phenomena were at work in this collapse: a religion that concentrated
on absolute power in a "divine" ruler; a compliant bureaucracy, loyal only to
its own existence; and a class of priests whose beliefs and rites were essential-
ly devoted to the welfare of a tiny elite.

Save for its faithful civil servants and their organization, the outcome was
the same as on the northern continent of the Americas: The substance and
the symbols of Inca civilization disappeared overnight like ashes scattered in
a high wind.

☾ THE PUEBLO INDIANS

When Coronado and his men climbed onto the Colorado Plateau looking for another Mexico, it was inevitable that they would regard the civilization of their hosts (whom they named the Pueblo, that is, "town," Indians) as backward and relatively primitive.

New Mexico: Puye ruins near Santa Clara Pueblo, occupied ca. 1250–1550

The initial contact left the Spaniards deeply disappointed. The "golden cities" of Cíbola were made of mud. There was no king; there was no splendid capital to conquer.

Yet, despite these shocks, the first impressions of the Spaniards were not all negative. The bulging granaries of the Zuni Indians saved them from starvation. They also surely admired the ingenious methods the Zunis were using to farm thousands of acres of lowlands with floodwaters from infrequent rains. And they must have respected the construction techniques that enabled the Zuni masons to build multistoried dwellings that compared favorably with some Aztec architecture.

But the writings of Coronado and his soldiers suggest that it was the orderliness and cohesion of Pueblo culture that won their highest esteem. In his letter to the king, Coronado noted that the Zunis were "intelligent" and praised their dignity and well-ordered lives while Pedro de Castañeda made these observations about their social behavior:

> *They do not have chiefs as in New Spain, but are ruled by*
> *a council of the oldest men. They have priests who preach to*
> *them . . . [who] go up on the highest roof of the village and*
> *preach to the village from there, like public criers, in the*
> *morning while the sun is rising, the whole village being*
> *silent and sitting in the galleries to listen. They tell them*
> *how to live, and I believe that they give certain command-*
> *ments for them to keep, for there is no drunkenness among*
> *them nor sodomy nor sacrifices, neither do they eat flesh*
> *nor steal, but they are usually at work.*

Respect would have ripened had the Spaniards taken the time to learn how the religion and "lifeways" of these industrious Indians were interwoven with their rituals and ceremonies. The Zunis' conduct was well ordered because their religion held that personal fulfillment would be found through family unity and communal happiness. There was no place in their religion for Aztecan displays of power or for "kings" or "nobles" or powerful priests.

The Pueblo people that Coronado and his companions studied were in constant communion with the natural world. Harmony was a central theme of their worship: They sought harmony with nature, harmony with other Indian groups, harmony with the members of their own villages. The social goals the Pueblos distilled out of centuries of living in a demanding environment were amity, not conquest; stability, not strife; conservation, not waste; restraint, not aggression.

Restraint, we know now, is a constant of the Pueblo religion. Coronado witnessed its influence, and the persistence of Pueblo culture attests to the wisdom and strength of this concept. It has preserved the independent village pattern of Pueblo life for centuries; it has damped combative impulses and dissuaded any village from seeking dominion over other Pueblos or other Indian groups; and, above all, it has prevented the appearance of ego-centered "strong men."

Arizona: The Hopi village of Walpi, built after the Pueblo Revolt of 1680

Restraint has enabled these sturdy Indians to keep their culture substantially intact during the advent of padres, Spanish colonizers, marauding Apaches, cavalrymen, Protestant missionaries—and, in more recent times, a well-meaning Great Society, the automobile, and even television.

It is the sustainability of Pueblo culture that permits us in the 1990s to argue thus: The most compelling indigenous group encountered by the conquistadores in the New World, the one that has the most to say to our troubled world, was not the Aztecs or the Incas but the Indians whom Coronado contacted in the north. The triumph of this society for all seasons cannot be attributed to its location in an inaccessible region of the Americas. The Pueblo

New Mexico: Picuris Pueblo

Indians lived face-to-face for more than two centuries with the same Spanish power that overwhelmed native cultures in Mexico and Latin America. In addition, they have maintained the core of their way of life against the inordinate pressures of a dynamic U.S. civilization.

In their dignified way, are these people making a statement to other cultures? Does their example of sustained accommodation, one wonders, say something profound to their fellow Americans—and to quarreling countries that must learn to live together or die?

Perhaps it is time to pause and ponder whether some of the supposed "primitive" societies were so backward after all. Even in Coronado's time,

Pueblo culture was not as underdeveloped as the Spaniards supposed. Five centuries earlier, Puebloan ancestors had built a vast network/civilization radiating from Chaco Canyon, in New Mexico, including a huge apartment house that was probably the largest dwelling structure in the world. These were pragmatic people. They would have been critical of the great pyramids and temples built by the Aztecs and the Incas. Their religious shrines were the majestic mesas and buttes and mountains that surrounded them. It was, and is, their conviction that human energy should be used to promote life, to care for the primal needs of people.

Only in this century have our own experts in the arts begun to recognize the contributions of the Pueblo people. It was the eminent art historian Vincent Scully who wrote these words after he came to the Southwest and studied the art woven into the life of the Pueblo Indians:

> *The dances themselves I believe to be the most profound*
> *works of art yet produced on the American continent. They*
> *call up a pity and terror which only Greek tragedy rivals,*
> *no less than a comic joy, at once animal and ironic, that*
> *suggests the precursors of Aristophanes. And to the begin-*
> *nings of Greek drama they are, I believe, fundamentally*
> *allied in a comparative sense.*

Does the example of the Puebloan people say something about the sustainability of empires and the ambitions of "great powers"? Why, they seem to ask, did mankind ever admire the evanescent "conquests" of the Tamerlanes and Napoleons and Moctezumas of the world? Their history exemplifies the lesson that, in the long run, aggressive behavior is self-destructive.

Coronado's Forerunners

*The story of Cabeza de Vaca is incredible and would have
to be considered myth except that it is true.*
—BERNARD DEVOTO
The Course of Empire

◖ CABEZA DE VACA

His name, Alvar Núñez Cabeza de Vaca, flows like the
sound of a freshet working its way across a bed of rocks. He and his three
companions were the first Europeans to study the vast interior of the continental United States. What makes the saga of Cabeza de Vaca unforgettable
is that he and his comrades did not penetrate inland and wander about from
eastern Texas to Sonora as armed conquerors or amateur students of geography;
rather, they came barefoot as "white Indians" drifting with "savage" friends,
searching for signs of a civilization they had lost.

These four were the only survivors of a pretentious, four-hundred-man
expedition under Pánfilo Narváez that had put ashore near Tampa Bay, Florida,
in April 1528. Cabeza de Vaca, their leader, was a nobleman, born at Jerez de
la Frontera, in the wine country near Cádiz. Vaca's grandfather, Pedro de Vera,
was a legendary Spaniard who had conquered Grand Canary Island. He had
friends in the royal court and had embarked with Narváez, as the king's treasurer and high sheriff of this ill-fated expedition.

The other survivors were Captain Alfonso de Castillo, son of a Salamanca
physician; Andrés Dorantes, of Bejar; and an African, Esteban, who was a
native of Azamor, in Morocco, and who is identified in various reports as "the
Moor" and "an Arabian black."

The appearance of these four scarecrows near Culiacán, on the west coast
of Mexico, in 1536 was a cause for wonder. There was an aura of Lazarus
about these men, for their entrada had long since vanished into the mists of
New World history. They brought an account of a feckless colonizing expedi-

tion that was doomed almost from the day the inept Pánfilo Narváez ordered a landing in the swamplands of Florida. They told of a leader who did not lead, of support ships that disappeared, of food supplies that lasted only a few days, of desperate efforts to paddle across the Gulf of Mexico in crude boats, of shipwrecks on the Texas coast, and of merciful Indians who kept some of them alive during a first winter of quiet terror and hunger that turned some men into cannibals.

Out of the four hundred, what enabled these four to endure? The devout Alvar Núñez ascribed their survival to ". . . the power and mercy of God." However, the story he told to the new viceroy of Mexico suggests that their deity gave these castaways exceptional traits that allowed them to adapt, to shed their European memories, and to learn the survival skills of the coastal aborigines who were their masters and companions.

Plainly, these four men had a tenacious will to live that the others lacked. Even so, Cabeza de Vaca's writings also intimate that these four lived because they had had a sensitivity and humility that allowed them to look into the eyes of their hosts and see their own humanity. They became brothers who learned to share Indian joys and participate as equals in everyday Indian existence.

Life with the coastal natives ended, Alvar Núñez tells us, when the four arranged a rendezvous and decided to move toward the setting sun with friendly inland Indians. They had no sense of the vast reach of the region they were entering. But it was time to take some risks, time to find out if there was a "land bridge" that might take them to the New Spain conquered by Hernán Cortés.

The initial guides of this gypsy hegira to the west were nomadic Indians who subsisted by harvesting the seasonal foods (nuts, cactus fruits, roots, berries, wild game) found in these semiarid uplands. In our century, admirers of Alvar Núñez have been able to reconstruct his route largely through the landscapes and subsistence foods he described in his story.

Their trek into the interior of Texas began when they tagged along with some natives who traveled up a "River of Nuts" to feast on pecans. This, experts tell us, is a clear portrayal of the valley of the Colorado River of Texas, and it seems likely the Spaniards wintered over in the vicinity of Austin, where they became the first foreigners to see herds of buffalo. Next, they went along with their hosts on a summer harvest trip among the *tuna* (prickly pear) thickets in the area of San Antonio.

But this wandering seemed aimless, and Cabeza de Vaca says his group broke away again, returned to the River of Nuts, and fell in with another band of Indians heading for its winter lodges near the confluence of the Colorado and the Concho rivers, below San Angelo.

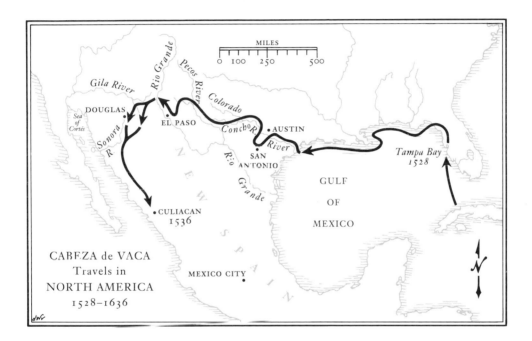

Here there was a magical development that transformed their status and made the rest of their journey a sort of triumphal procession: The Spaniards began ministering to sick Indians and effected cures, which made them shamans in the eyes of the natives. Now these Indians with white skin were medicine men, and as word of the power of their curative prayers raced ahead of them, they were welcomed wherever they went, and their journey became a kind of ambulatory Lourdes in the wilderness. It was now, if not earlier, that the king's treasurer became a confirmed Indian lover and acquired the affection for aborigines that colored the remaining years of his life.

Now their pathway was paved by Indian welcoming committees: As they were passed from clan to clan, guides who knew that they wanted to move onward toward the setting sun were ready and willing to help. Now their walk became purposeful as they passed over the Concho watershed, worked their way up the valley of the Pecos River to Elk Creek, climbed a pine-clad ridge (where piñon nuts added a delicacy to their diets), and descended into the green valley of New Mexico's Tularosa River.

Here there was a puzzling detour along the edge of the Sacramento Mountains to the Great River below El Paso. But when the western wishes of the Spaniards were asserted again, the Indians guided them up the east side of the Rio Grande by Las Cruces to a ford at Rincon. There they waded across to a western trail that skirted the flanks of the Mogollon Mountains.

There are continuing arguments about the final leg of De Vaca's walk in what is now the United States. Was he guided into Arizona by going up Berrenda Creek to the basin of the Mimbres River? Did he then cross over the Burro Mountains to the Gila River and up the San Simon River to the pass between the Chiricahua and Dos Cabezas mountains and on to Douglas, Arizona? Or, as others would have it, did he follow an alternate Indian trail that remained in New Mexico along the eastern side of the rugged Peloncillo range? Whatever ultimately may be the right answer to this trail mystery, we know that Alvar Núñez and his companions arrived with a large contingent of camp followers in the Sonora Valley home of the Opata Indians in the "land of maize."

There rumors of a nearby ocean crept into the conversations, and the men of Spain must have realized their ordeal might soon end. The path went due south, and expectations quickened until one day, in Sinaloa, the treasurer spotted something more precious than gold: a Spanish horseshoe nail worn as an amulet around the neck of an approaching Indian.

The wanderers "gave many thanks to God" when they learned they were in country where "Christians on horses" had recently traveled. With an escort of eleven natives, De Vaca and Esteban raced ahead, found three villages where the Christians had camped, and soon caught up with "four of them." The scarecrows clothed in animal skins spoke to these Spaniards, who were "confounded" and simply stared at them for "a length of time."

This strange reunion had a shameful twist that the treasurer remembered with bitterness when he wrote his report to the king. He had stumbled onto "Christians" who were on a slave-catching expedition—and as soon as he turned his back, they began capturing his Indian friends. Alvar Núñez says he rebuked his countrymen and demanded that his followers be allowed to live in these valleys unmolested. However, he surely must have wondered as he continued on the road back to civilization whether his wishes were obeyed.

The odyssey of Cabeza de Vaca and his friends will beguile us as long as exploration is a subject of fascination. These men were the first to cross what is now the United States "from sea to sea," and they were the first to provide Europe with baseline information about the scope and size of the interior landmass of North America. Moreover, it was the rumors they brought about "opulent countries" north of their trail that set wheels turning and, four years later, produced the exploring expedition led by Francisco Vázquez de Coronado.

In addition to geography, Cabeza de Vaca brought truths about white/Indian relationships that might have changed the course of North American settlement had leaders been willing to listen. Seven years' experience had taught him the paramount truth that Europeans and American Indians could live and work together if people were adaptable and if the newcomers with lighter skins made an effort to comprehend Indian values and explore the possibilities of brotherly behavior. Necessity had also taught Alvar Núñez the corollary to this truth: American Indians were not inferior savages or children but human beings developing differently who had the same drives and dreams and intelligence and emotions as the Europeans.

This agonizing truth was to hover over—and haunt—the whole sad story of the settlement of North America. Tragically, however, this verity never entered the main currents of thought. But, over the centuries, by chance, other De Vacas appeared who won victories that helped some Indian cultures to survive. Among the other Cabeza de Vacas who learned to understand and work with Indians were several generations of New Mexico padres, Captain Juan de Anza, Arizona's Father Kino, New Mexico's Governor Diego de Vargas, Brigham Young's Indian peacemaker Jacob Hamblin (my great-grandfather) —and that singular U.S. general who loved Indians, George Crook.

Alvar Núñez Cabeza de Vaca sprinkled hints about his anger, and about the strength of his Indian convictions, in the report he sent to his king. Happily, four centuries later, a southwestern poet, Haniel Long, composed a prose poem in an effort to evoke the message hidden between the lines of this report. Long's eloquent little book *The Power Within Us* was an epitaph for De Vaca. It grips us now because the author's words distill old truths mankind has never learned but never completely forgotten:

> *. . . Your Majesty, since I addressed you first, you have become more mysterious to me and more majestic, and this increases my sense of freedom in speaking to you. To the understanding of such days and events this additional narrative becomes necessary, like a real figure to walk beside a ghost.*
>
> *Your Majesty will remember my indignation in my first narrative, that Christians should be so wicked, especially such as had the advantages of being your subjects. I did not at the time understand the true source of my indignation. I do now, and I will explain it. In facing these marauders I was compelled to face the Spanish gentleman I myself had been eight years before. It was not easy to think of it. Andrés and Alfonso agreed that it was not easy. What, your Majesty, is so melancholy as to confront one's former unthinking and unfeeling self?*
>
> *Our journey westward was but a long series of encounters. Your Majesty, encounters have become my meditation. The moment one accosts a stranger or is accosted by him is above all in this life the moment of drama. The eyes of Indians who have crossed my trail have searched me to the very depths to estimate my power. It is true the world over. It is true of a Spaniard meeting another on the road between Toledo and Salamanca. Whoever we meet watches us intently at the quick strange moment of meeting, to see whether we are disposed to be friendly.*

*While with them I thought only about doing the
Indians good. But back among my fellow countrymen, I had
to be on my guard not to do them positive harm. If one lives
where all suffer and starve, one acts on one's own impulse
to help. But where plenty abounds, we surrender our gen-
erosity, believing that our country replaces us each and several. This is not so, and indeed a delusion. On the contrary
the power of maintaining life in others, lives within each of
us, and from each of us does it recede when unused. It is a
concentrated power. If you are not acquainted with it, your
Majesty can have no inkling of what it is like, what it por-
tends, or the ways in which it slips from one.*
    In the name of God, your Majesty, Farewell.

Incredibly, the story of Cabeza de Vaca did not end when he returned to
Spain. He had such esteem in high places that he obtained a royal commission
that made him governor of the province of Río de la Plata, with authority
over half of the western world south of the equator. The new governor then
organized men and ships in Spain, landed in 1540 on the coast of Brazil, and
in 1542 led a thousand-mile walk across a wilderness in southern Brazil to
Asunción. There he instituted a humane Indian policy. But his rule was short-
lived. Rivals who regarded him as "soft on Indians" mounted a rebellion,
trumped up charges, and sent him home in chains to wage a losing fight for
his honor. Like so many westering Spaniards of his generation, Alvar Núñez
Cabeza de Vaca spent the last years of his existence in poverty and disgrace.

No sixteenth-century Spaniard gave more of himself to his king—or to
humanity—than Alvar Núñez. As an explorer of undiscovered country, he
stands on a pinnacle alone. He gave "two lives" to the New World: He is
unforgettable as an Indian man—and his prodigious walks on two continents
will never be surpassed.

☾ ESTEBAN AND FRAY MARCOS

Before Cabeza de Vaca appeared with his rumors about rich cities, conquistadores were pursuing hunches that there was another Mexico in the north. Ensconced on an *estancia* in Oaxaca, Hernán Cortés had already financed a seaborne expedition that established a short-lived colony on an island near the Baja California peninsula, and scouting parties sent out by the aggressive governor of New Galicia, Nuño de Guzmán, had penetrated to the southern part of Sonora.

But the quests of these men would never be consummated, for their leeway to explore was circumscribed after King Carlos sent his own man, Don Antonio de Mendoza, to be the first viceroy of New Spain. Mendoza was a new-broom administrator, and he was directed to curb the power of the old-line conquistadores.

Don Antonio was a cautious man, instinctively skeptical of rumors emanating from his frontiers. After questioning de Vaca and his companions, he decided not to send a full-fledged military force to the northland until scouts under his personal control had performed a quiet reconnaissance. His first plan involved sending the castaways, Dorantes and Esteban, back up their old trail to carry out this investigation. For some reason, however, this effort aborted, and the viceroy was forced to recruit someone to replace Dorantes.

The person ultimately chosen was a Franciscan priest who had been with the conquistadores in Peru and Guatemala. He was a Frenchman from Nice who enjoyed the esteem of the archbishop of Mexico. History knows this man as Fray Marcos de Niza. His assignment was to lead a small, surreptitious walking party that could live off the land and bring back a private report to the viceroy. The guide selected to go with Marcos was the exuberant young man from Morocco, Esteban.

This unusual exploring team began the first leg of its mission in the early spring of 1539 by accompanying the recently appointed governor of New Galicia, Francisco Vázquez de Coronado, on an inspection visit to his northernmost city, Culiacán.

Fray Marcos reappeared alone in Mexico City five months later to report that he had been to a place called Cíbola and had seen an Indian community "larger than the City of Mexico," which had houses ten stories high, their doorways decorated with turquoise. Marcos also related that Indians who knew the area had told him all of Cíbola's Seven Cities had quantities of gold.

The friar had encouraged the lithe Esteban to plunge ahead with his Indian friends into the wilderness—but the Moor had been slain by angry Indians at the first of the Cíbolan cities. Marcos said he arrived in the area later, surveyed this city from a nearby hill, then fled "with much more fear than food."

It is not fair to picture Fray Marcos as a prevaricator. He saw no precious metals—and all he reported was that some Indians had informed him that the natives of the Seven Cities had unspecified quantities of gold. What followed is a classic study of the process by which the chemistry of human interactions transmutes rumors into facts. Marcos had the built-in Franciscan contempt for gold and money. It was not he but restless Spaniards inflamed with gold fever who created the flamboyant myth of the seven golden cities.

There is evidence Mendoza had serious reservations after he questioned Fray Marcos, for he quickly sent a party of scouts north under Melchor Díaz, the *alcalde* (mayor) of Culiacán, to gather more information about Cíbola and its supposed wealth. However, gold fever was so rampant in Mexico City that Mendoza had no choice but to send an expedition into the field to forestall similar action by Cortés or Pedro de Alvarado.

Many field investigators who have studied Fray Marcos's report and tried to match it with the geography of the region he traversed have decided that in all likelihood the friar did not travel as far north as the present Arizona border. If this judgment is sound, it leads to a conclusion that the famous Expedition of Fray Marcos de Niza should be renamed the Expedition of Esteban. The Zuni Indians told Coronado that Esteban arrived in their country, so it was the African, not Marcos, who was the first outsider to set foot in Arizona and New Mexico and to penetrate into the fastnesses of the Colorado Plateau.

Who was this remarkable pioneer? For centuries there has been confusion about his identity. The only thing we know for sure is that he was a native of Azamor in Morocco. The writers of the Coronado chronicles variously depicted him as a "Negro slave," an "Arabian black," and a Christianized Moor. Diego de Guzmán, who saw him at Sinaloa, created further confusion when he used the words "brown man" to describe his visage. But Esteban's skin color and religion are not the critical facts. What is vital is that we accord this man the recognition he has long been denied.

We need also to dispel the lingering myth that Esteban was a "Negro slave." This charismatic man may have been under some kind of servitude to Dorantes when he landed in Florida with the Narváez expedition in 1528, but, in reality, he was a free man when the remnants of that exploring party were capsized on the coast of Texas. Starving men trying to survive always stand on equal footing: There are no slaves or servants in a wilderness environment where individuals must adapt or perish.

The tenacity and inner strength of Esteban the Moor is attested to by the fact that only four of the four hundred men who went ashore with Narváez lived to tell the story of that tragic, ill-planned expedition. He is our only pioneer who made two long walks, not one, into the pages of U.S. history.

His story, of course, leaves us with an irony that still hovers over the Coronado entrada. Had Esteban's usual magic with Indians not failed him at Zuni—and had he lived to render a factual report about the natives of Cíbola to Viceroy Mendoza—would there have been a Coronado expedition? And if no entrada had been mounted in 1540, how much time would have elapsed before the southwestern quadrant of the United States was explored? Obviously there are no answers to these questions. Death silenced the Moor, and Fray Marcos's report was transformed overnight into a myth that became the engine that propelled the Coronado expedition on its way in the spring of 1540.

Finally, it is important to recognize that Fray Marcos, a supervisor of Franciscan affairs in Mexico, was a "... regular priest, pious, endowed with all virtues and dedication." Marcos was undoubtedly a visionary who perceived Spanish exploration as an activity that would open new vineyards for his missionaries. It is therefore sardonic that writers turned this simple man into the promoter of a great gold rush, when he and the members of his order had renounced worldly things and embraced a life-style dedicated to the idea that gold impeded the saving of human souls.

CORONADO'S
EXPLORATIONS
Mexico 1540

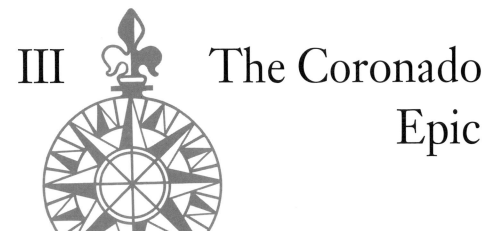

III The Coronado Epic

The Send-Off at Compostela

*[It was] the most brilliant company ever assembled
in the Indies to go in search of new lands.*
—PEDRO CASTAÑEDA

☾ THE POWER STRUGGLE

Mexico City, the nerve center of power in New Spain, was
an ingrown, gossipy capital. Consequently, Fray Marcos's "secret" report to
Viceroy Mendoza about the gilded cities of Cíbola was soon public knowledge.
This report—and the wild rumors it spawned—quickly provoked a power
struggle among conquistadores that reached all the way to Seville.

Don Antonio de Mendoza won this test of wills. Armed with the king's
most recent commission, he was able to dominate the decision-making process and personally launch the last great exploring parties of the Spanish age
of discovery. In a matter of months, Mendoza ended Cortés's New World
career, organized the Coronado expedition, and made a deal with Pedro de
Alvarado that enabled him to send Cabrillo and Villalobos on seaborne missions that put the stamp of Spanish power on the rim of the Pacific Ocean.

A cautious administrator ("Do nothing, and do it slowly" was one of his slogans), the viceroy realized Fray Marcos's message demanded decisive action. Mendoza had been in power four years and was ready to make important decisions without seeking additional authority from his superiors. A count who was a cousin of the powerful archbishop of Seville, Don Antonio was handpicked by the king to bring order to the affairs of New Spain—and to keep a wary eye on the schemes of Cortés and other old-line conquistadores.

It had been almost two decades since Cortés first arrived at the gates of Tenochtitlán. However, the aging eagle was still on the scene (bearing the honorific title "Marquis of the Valley") and probably learned the news Fray Marcos imparted to Mendoza in a matter of hours. With an eye on his old contract with the crown, which gave him a license to conquer "the north country," the restless conqueror naturally felt he was the logical leader to breach the gates of this new Eldorado. Cortés was a force the viceroy would have to reckon with: He had great wealth; and he was ready, once again, to use his skills to manipulate events.

Never averse to stealing a march on rivals, even before Mendoza arrived in New Spain Cortés was sending small ships up the west coast to search for Indians with precious metals. Indeed, even as Fray Marcos was returning to Mexico City, a flotilla led by Cortés's relative Francisco de Ulloa was making history. It discovered the Gulf of California, penetrated to the mouth of the Colorado River—and attached his name to the Sea of Cortés (the Gulf of California).

Cortés did not dally once he realized history was blowing in the wind. In August 1539, he made a lunge for the leadership of the Cíbola expedition. The "Marquis" first approached Mendoza with a partnership proposal that included an offer to finance the entire venture. When this was rejected, Cortés tried to persuade Coronado to intervene on his behalf. But when the viceroy (who was contemplating leading the expedition himself) growled a final "No," the New World career of Hernán Cortés came to an abrupt conclusion. Furious, the Marquis of the Valley went home to present a futile appeal to the Council of the Indies and never returned to the New World. He died a few years later at his castle near Seville.

Cortés's withdrawal did not alleviate Mendoza's anxieties. He knew that if he failed to get an entrada in the field, De Soto and Pedro de Alvarado would assert claims that might persuade the council to thwart his expedition.

Ignorance of geography—and the vagueness of the "hunting licenses" issued to various conquistadores—put Mendoza in a bind. In the 1530s the contours of the North American landmass were shrouded in uncertainty: The presumption that the land bridge between the East and the West was probably a "narrow waist" was so prevalent that, a few years earlier, Verrazano, in the pay of France, mistook the Chesapeake Bay for the Pacific Ocean.

This ambiguity invited aggressive men such as De Soto and Alvarado (the conqueror of Guatemala) to have their spokesmen in Seville argue that they had already been authorized to find the Seven Cities. The ambitious Alvarado had secured an elastic document from the Council of the Indies in 1537 giving him the right to explore "the coast of New Spain northward." Knowing he was in a race with formidable rivals, Alvarado gathered artisans and equipment and hauled heavy loads of hardware across the isthmus of Mexico. By the summer of 1539, he had a team of shipwrights at Iztapa building the largest fleet ever assembled by Spaniards on the Pacific coast.

Hernando de Soto, grizzled veteran of the Aztec and Inca campaigns, had also procured a flexible commission, in 1537, that authorized him to explore and colonize "Florida" (an ill-defined area stretching indefinitely westward from the Atlantic Ocean). De Soto had left Spain for Florida in 1538 with a force of six hundred men, and his agents in Seville could logically contend that he had been on the mainland for many months and might soon arrive in the vicinity of Cíbola. It would be wasteful, they argued, to send competing expeditions into the same region.

A De Soto who had vanished into a wilderness could not prevail against the king's viceroy. However, when Pedro de Alvarado moved his new ships up the Pacific coast to Navidad in the autumn of 1540 (about the time Coronado's discouraging report from Cíbola was delivered to Mendoza) and went inland to parley, he was poised to strike a bargain with Mendoza. We do not know whether Don Antonio told Alvarado about the bad news from Hawikuh, but their agreement to explore the northland together fell into

Mendoza's lap when Alvarado was killed a few months later in an Indian uprising known as the Mixtón War.

The sturdy ships Alvarado built and Don Antonio inherited did not bring immediate wealth into Spain's coffers. They did, though, trace imperishable lines on the world's new maps: One of those sailing ships carried Mendoza's brother-in-law, Ruy Gómez de Villalobos, on a new route across the Pacific to the Philippines, opening the door to the transpacific trade of the Manila Galleon's famous ships. Other boats assembled by Alvarado's artisans carried Cabrillo and Ferrelo on the first European seaborne search up the Pacific coast to Oregon.

Mendoza initiated these voyages later, but in the fall of 1539 he concentrated his energies on organizing the best-prepared expedition Spain would ever send into unknown country. Vital decisions were made with dispatch: He and his friends would finance the venture (to avoid a request for royal assistance); he would recruit high-quality officers and soldiers; and he would ask his closest friend, the twenty-nine-year-old governor, Francisco Vázquez de Coronado, to be the captain general.

The organizing efforts of Mendoza and Vázquez de Coronado (who put a large part of his wife's dowry into the pot) culminated in an unusual muster/ send-off ceremony on February 22, 1540, on the town square of the city of Compostela, five hundred miles northwest of the capital of New Spain. It was the only time a written muster roll was taken of departing conquistadores, the only instance of an army of explorers being supervised by a viceroy of Spain.

☾ THE MUSTER ROLL

We know a lot about events that day at Compostela— exactly 192 years before George Washington was born in 1732—because Don Antonio had issued an order that each soldier would pass before an inspector and declare his possessions. Thus, diligent scribes recorded the names and ages of those who went and the attire and equipment they took with them. One entry tells us that in addition to his "gilded suit and helmet with crested plume," Coronado took twenty-three horses and three or four suits of horse armor. Another informs us that Captain Cárdenas had twelve horses, three sets of Castilian armor, two pair of cuirasses (metal vests), and a coat of mail. And a third notation states that young Juan Gallego (who would earn his spurs as a member of the first team of "pony express" riders in what is now the United States) checked in with "seven horses, a crossbow, a coat of mail with breeches, a buckskin coat . . . and other Castillian and native weapons."

Additional entries convey the information that

- Captain Don Tristán de Luna y Arellano carried a wide array of armor and weapons that included a leather jacket, sleeves and neckpieces of mail, "arms of the country" (that is, native-made weapons and/or vests), a chin piece, a harquebus, two crossbows, a two-handed sword, three ordinary swords, and other assorted arms for himself and his servants;

- Hernando de Alvarado (a relative of Don Pedro) was a twenty-three-year-old stripling who checked in with four horses and a coat of mail with sleeves;

- the second in command, Campmaster Lope de Samaniego (who would be the first to die when an Indian arrow pierced his eye), reported sixteen horses, two buckskin jackets, a coat of mail, some cuirasses, and arms of the country; and

- then there was the downtrodden enlisted man Juan de Vegara, a cavalryman, who declared that the only animal he had to ride was a mule.

The official roll lists 225 mounted men and 62 foot soldiers. When one adds those who had gone ahead, Coronado commanded a force of 336 soldiers. The muster also includes some surprises, as all of these adventurers were not male Spaniards. In addition to five Portuguese enlistees who made the long trip to Cíbola, there were two Italians, a Frenchman, a Scot, and a German (the bugler, Juan Fisch) plus three intrepid women, Francisca de Hozes (the wife of the shoemaker), María Maldonado (who became the expedition's nurse), and the native wife of Lope Caballero.

On foot in the front rank were Fray Marcos and four Franciscan padres —and bringing up the rear were seven hundred "Indian allies" who went along as servants, wranglers, and herdsmen of the sheep, horses, and cattle brought along for food and transport.

The muster roll and other documents also provide data that allow us to develop profiles of some of the marchers in this last New World entrada. Let us familiarize ourselves with some of these characters before we follow them up the trail to the Seven Cities of Cíbola:

Francisco Vázquez de Coronado (whose true family name was Vázquez, not Coronado, in accordance with Spanish custom) was the second son of a noble family of Salamanca. He would soon be thirty. One of his younger brothers, Juan, later came to Mexico and became the first governor of Costa Rica; a second brother, Pedro, was in the retinue of King Felipe II when he went to England, in 1554, to marry Queen Mary. Soon after Coronado came to New Spain with Mendoza, he married Beatriz de Estrada, a daughter of the deceased royal treasurer of Mexico, Alonso de Estrada. (Estrada, a wealthy man, made no secret of the fact that he was a son "on the wrong side of the blanket" of none other than King Ferdinand himself.) Coronado had served as governor of a province and as a troop commander in Indian campaigns, and he was named to the town council of Mexico City before Mendoza appointed him captain general.

Lope de Samaniego, the ill-starred deputy commander, also a veteran of Indian campaigns, had recently been in charge of the royal arsenal in Mexico City.

Don García López de Cárdenas, another young noble, was a favorite of the viceroy who had performed important work for Mendoza.

Don Tristán de Arellano, the captain who commanded the main force after Samaniego's death, earned such high marks on this entrada that he was chosen to lead a colonizing expedition to Florida in 1559.

Hernando de Alarcón, discoverer and first explorer of the Colorado River, had served as the viceroy's chamberlain. His seaborne expedition was a success, but he failed to carry out orders to link up with and supply the land army. Obscurity surrounds his subsequent life.

Hernando de Alvarado, one of the outstanding outriders of the expedition (first to reach Acoma, Tigüex, Taos, Pecos, and the buffalo plains), had been in New Spain since his youth and had previously served under the command of Cortés.

Juan de Zaldivar, an outstanding scout, was related to the Oñate family. If he had lived to a ripe old age, he would have seen one of his kinfolk, Juan de Oñate, found the first permanent settlement in New Mexico in 1598.

Melchor Díaz was a much-admired commoner who became the most trusted, most beloved captain of all. Little is known of his origins, but Díaz was mayor of Culiacán when Cabeza de Vaca and his scarecrows turned up. The discriminating De Vaca went out of his way to praise the character of Mayor Díaz.

Pablo de Melgosa was a wiry young captain of the footmen. We will meet him on the road as the leader of the climbers who tried to descend into the Grand Canyon from its South Rim.

Don Rodrigo Maldonado was a cavalry captain who was a close friend of Coronado's. Maldonado led a side trip to the Pacific Ocean, went to Quivira, and was in a horse race with Coronado when the girth on Coronado's saddle broke, nearly killing him as a hoof struck his head.

Among the rank and file, there were also colorful characters who deserve special mention, such as

Francisco Santillán, blacksmith/veterinarian who received an arrow wound on the Rio Grande and was sent home an invalid;

Alfonso Manrique de Lara, a rolling stone from Valladolid who had served his country earlier in Buenos Aires, Tabasco, and the Yucatán;

Diego López, a former alderman of Seville;

Cristóbal de Quesada, an artist who went along "to paint the things of the country" but whose canvases did not survive the centuries; and

Tomás Blaque (*Blake*), a Scottish veteran of earlier campaigns, who was apparently the only Briton (and surely a devout Catholic!) allowed to become a citizen of New Spain during this period.

The "journalists" of this expedition also deserve special mention. They included:

Coronado himself, whose dispatches to the viceroy and the king were preserved;

Juan Jaramillo, a veteran of wars in Italy and Tunis. Jaramillo became a captain and, years afterward, composed a brief but invaluable account of events along "the turquoise trail";

Pedro de Castañeda was a foot soldier who had a way with words. Castañeda remained in Culiacán when the returning army passed by. In his old age (like Bernal Díaz, who wrote the best memoir of Cortés and his conquests), he wrote the account of the Coronado campaign that contains the most revealing details; and

Don Pedro de Tovar, the chief standard-bearer, or ensign, is famous as the discoverer of the Hopi country. Tovar was a younger son of a Spanish noble in whom it is evident King Carlos reposed great trust. His father was the "lord high steward and guardian," at a prison castle on a hillside near Tordesillas, of the legendary demented queen mother, Juana la Loca. Don Pedro apparently wrote an account of his experiences and left it with the Franciscans in Culiacán. Tovar's papers were used by the historian Mota Padilla two hundred years later but disappeared thereafter.

Finally, we need to pay attention to the sandal-shod Franciscans who were already on the trail ahead of Coronado. All Franciscan friars were dogged walkers because St. Francis of Assisi forbade his followers to ride horses, as they were symbols of nobility and wealth. In addition to the enigmatic Fray Marcos (who made a hasty retreat to Mexico after the fiasco at Cíbola), there were the following:

Fray Juan de Padilla, a rugged Andalusian whose decade of missionary work had taken him from the Isthmus of Panama to Tepic. The venturesome Padilla was usually in the vanguard: He took the first tour of New Mexico with Alvarado and traveled all the way to Kansas with Coronado. Later we will follow his final walk, to martyrdom among the Indians of Quivira;

Fray Antonio de Victoria, the chaplain of the expedition, was also in the forefront. He influenced Coronado's decisions about handling conflicts with

Indians. This Franciscan also stayed behind. In due course, we will pick up
the story of his final days; and

Luis de Escalona, a friar who was listed as a "former companion" of the
lord bishop of Mexico, the eminent Juan de Zumárraga.

The main reason the padres were in the vanguard—and were usually
consulted about Indian questions—was that the viceroy wanted it that way.
The devout Mendoza knew the mind of his king—and was a friend of Bishop
Bartolomé de Las Casas, the great champion of Indian humanity. Mendoza
was determined, as Archbishop Zumárraga reported to his superiors in Spain,
that this mission of conquest would ". . . be Christian and apostolic and not a
butchery." This helps explain why Mendoza chose Coronado, why he issued
orders that the Indians they encountered be ". . . treated as if they were Spaniards," and why he directed that the "Indian allies" not be used as *tamenes*
(carriers) for the caravan.

This latter fiat had serious consequences. In his very first dispatch, Coronado reported to Mendoza that ". . . soldiers of high rank [were] going on
foot because they carried their food and other belongings on their horses."
Indeed, to attest to his own brand of leadership, Coronado reminded Don
Antonio that he had set an example on many occasions by dismounting and
walking with his men ". . . so soldiers who were thus traveling laden would
suffer and withstand the hardships with greater fortitude."

There are many signs that the devout Mendoza put the missionary aims
of his expedition on a par with the search for mines and precious metals.
Mendoza saw himself as a reformer: The Indian orders he issued were clear
and stern.

Having made the long journey to Compostela to put his personal stamp on
the expedition, the viceroy wanted some open-air pageantry to stir loyalties
and impress these soldier/pilgrims with the solemnity of their mission. It was
Sunday, so he ordered a parade. A mass was celebrated by Father Victoria.
Then the viceroy gave ". . . a very eloquent short speech" in which he stressed
the importance of fidelity to God, to the king, and to their commander—and
envisioned the "benefits" for everyone if the venture was a success.

Finally, after a swearing-in ceremony for Coronado, each soldier presented himself to the chaplain, placed his right hand on a cross and a prayer book, and "in a loud voice" took an oath "to uphold the service of God and his Majesty . . . [and to] be obedient to the said Francisco Vázquez de Coronado . . . as a gentleman should do to the best of his ability and intelligence."

Now the long march—the longest by any conquistadores in the sixteenth century—commenced. To lift their morale and underscore that this was *his* entrada, Viceroy Antonio de Mendoza rode down the trail for two days with his men.

Up from Mexico

THE PATH CORONADO and his companions followed for the next four months took them on an ecological tour of five differing life zones over terrain ranging from the semitropical, in Nayarit, to the alpine, on top of the White Mountains in Arizona. With their animals, they would climb eight thousand feet from marshes at sea level near San Blas and trudge across great expanses of the Sonoran Desert before they topped out in a ponderosa pine forest north of McNary, Arizona.

The trail from Compostela ran north through small, inviting valleys to Jalisco and Tepic to a crossing on the Santiago River. This lush country of banana trees, orange groves (transplanted from old Spain), bounteous gardens, and cascading streams was a misleading preview for the trekkers. Daydreams of this tropical paradise surely tantalized the minds of the wayfarers as they struggled through dusty gardens of cactus in the Sonoran Desert.

Rafts were needed to transport equipment and supplies at the Santiago ford. Cavalrymen were drafted for double duty when a decision was made to ferry the sheep across this alligator-infested river "one by one" on the saddles of the *caballeros*. Beyond the Santiago, the slow-moving caravan worked its way through dense jungles of brush on the coastal plain of Sinaloa along a

Arizona: "The Cordillera" (Pinaleno Mountains) near Chichilticale

*Arizona: Texas Canyon and
the Dragoon Mountains*

*Arizona: Gila Mountains
and Mount Turnbull from
Nantack Ridge*

Arizona: View of the Gila Mountains—beginning of the Despoblado

Arizona: Gila River and Mount Turnbull from the crest of the Gila Mountains

Arizona: Ash Flat on the San Carlos Apache Reservation

Arizona: Santa Teresa Mountains west of the Gila Valley

Arizona: Bonita Prairie

Arizona: Alligator-bark juniper. Bonita Prairie

Arizona: White Mountains near McNary

Arizona: View of the Grand Canyon from the South Rim

*New Mexico:
Towaya' Lane—
sacred mountain
where Zuni Indians
sought refuge from
the Spaniards*

New Mexico: Ventana Natural Arch, Cebollita Mesa, on the trail to Acoma

New Mexico: Malpaís (lava badlands) between Hawikuh and Acoma

New Mexico: Mesas on the Laguna Reservation along the trail to Tigüex

New Mexico:
Sky City
of Acoma
at sunset

New Mexico: Rio Grande Valley from a mesa near Santa Clara Pueblo

New Mexico: The Rio Grande Valley in winter from the Sangre de Cristo Mountains

New Mexico: Pecos Mission Church with kiva *(ceremonial chamber) in foreground*

New Mexico: Pecos River and Santa Fe Mountains from Glorieta Mesa

New Mexico: The Great River and sacred butte of San Ildefonso Indians

*New Mexico: The Sangre de Cristo
Mountains in the fall; from San
Juan Pueblo*

*New Mexico: Pecos River Gorge
above Anton Chico*

New Mexico: Inscription Rock, El Morro National Monument

New Mexico:
The Rio Grande
and the Sandia
Mountains from
the Tigüex village
of Kuaua

Texas: Caprock and eroded canyon walls, Triassic Peak, Palo Duro Canyon

Texas: Palo Duro Canyon east of city of Canyon

Texas: Palo Duro Canyon—Llano escarpment in the background

Texas: On the Llano Estacado east of Canyon

*New Mexico: Escarpment
of the Llano Estacado east
of Santa Rosa*

Texas: Panhandle east of Canyon

Texas: Elm Creek near Abilene

Texas: Valley of the Canadian River near Borger

Kansas: Wheat field west of Lindsborg

Texas: The Llano Estacado east of Wayside

*Kansas: Spring thunderstorm,
northeast of Lyons. Area of
sixteenth-century Quivira
council circles and the recently
discovered serpentine intaglio*

*Kansas: Kerger Creek
west of Ashland*

*Oklahoma: Cimarron River in the
Oklahoma Panhandle*

*Kansas: "Middle Spring"
in Cimarron National
Grassland on the
Cimarron cutoff of the
Santa Fe Trail*

route that probably paralleled the highway and railroad that today carry the commerce of that region.

In mid-March, at Chiametla, two sobering events occurred. Samaniego, the deputy commander, was killed while leading a foraging party. After the rebellious natives were punished, there was a moment of excitement when Coronado intercepted the scouts the viceroy had sent north to verify the Cíbola facts reported by Fray Marcos. Captain Melchor Díaz bore a written message for Mendoza, and his private report to the captain general surely raised doubts in Don Francisco's mind about the existence of golden cities. On the subject of gold, Díaz was blunt. He wrote: "They [his Indian informants] were also unable to tell me of any metal, nor did they say that they had it."

December snows had forced Díaz to halt and winter over at Chichilticale (the Red House). But after quizzing Indians who had been to Cíbola (including a native who had been one of Esteban's escorts), he was dubious about a bonanza of precious metals at the end of the northern trail. The report Díaz wrote for Viceroy Mendoza was so crisp and cogent that Don Antonio included most of it verbatim in a dispatch he forwarded to King Carlos on April 17, 1540. Melchor Díaz was an experienced frontiersman attuned to Indian nuances, and his portrayal of Cíbolan culture accurately described the outlines of a civilization he had not seen for a king he had not met.

As governor of New Galicia, Coronado had been exposed to Melchor Díaz's versatile competence. Before the long campaign was over, he would place heavy burdens on this man. On the spot, he ordered Díaz to turn about and become the point man of the expedition. Juan Zaldivar, his aide, was sent south to deliver the report to Mendoza.

Díaz also brought disturbing news that beyond the Red House there was a *despoblado* (unpopulated wilderness), where food was scarce. This prompted the captain general to make important decisions Easter week, when he arrived at Culiacán: He would lead a forced march to Cíbola with eighty horsemen and a small contingent of foot soldiers; the main force would inch forward under Arellano to a camp in the Valley of Hearts and await marching orders from its commander.

Now the pace quickened. Within a month, Don Francisco and his men followed Melchor Díaz on an inland route due north across the Fuerte, Mayo, and Yaqui rivers. Beyond the Río Yaqui, the rocks were sharper, and some ridges were so steep that horses died and many of the trailing lambs lost their hooves.

They were averaging twelve miles per day, and their arrival for a rest stop at Cabeza de Vaca's Valley of Hearts (near present-day Ures) was an occasion for rejoicing. Díaz announced they were approaching a beautiful section of the trail where they would be near water and move in the shade of deep canyons. This ride, through a region that contains some of Mexico's finest Coronado-scapes, wound through the scenic gorge of the Sonora River into an open valley of green fields farmed by Opata Indians. From there it continued to Babiácora, Senoquipe, Arizpe, and beyond to a junction where the west fork of the Sonora begins ascending to its headwater arroyos on the grasslands east of the modern mining town of Cananea.

At the crest of this watershed, a new, north-running stream (called the Nexpa by the Indians and the San Pedro by later Spanish settlers) begins. It was now late May. A day's travel down this freshet brought the conquistadores to an imaginary line that centuries later would be an international boundary. It would also take them to the foothills of the beautiful island-mountains, the Huachucas, which add ecological variety and visual splendor to the Sonoran uplands in southern Arizona—and which also provide one of the most diverse wildlife habitats in North America.

This part of the Sonoran Desert embraces unusual natural wonders. As he crossed it, Coronado and his companions were winding through creosote bushes, which have been recently identified by scientists as the oldest living plants on earth, some with a longevity of more than eleven thousand years. And some of the high peaks the Spaniards saw on their journeys nurture dwarfed bristlecone pine trees rated as the second-oldest growing things on our planet.

But there was no time to ponder nature's curiosities. All eyes were on the high country that loomed on the horizon.

Across Arizona to Hawikuh

In late may of 1540, the conquistadores entered what is now Arizona near the ranching town of Palominas, southeast of Tucson. The desert days were hot and dry, and it is a good bet the horsemen stayed close to the San Pedro River as they headed downstream. This narrow valley is framed by the pine-clad Huachuca Mountains on the west and the low ridges of the Mule Mountains on the east. (Most of the mountains the Spaniards skirted on their trek through southern Arizona are in a land unit designated today as the Coronado National Forest.)

One hundred and fifty years later, this valley attracted the interest of other Spaniards when it was part of a region dominated by roving bands of Apache Indians who entered the area after Coronado left. The great missionary Father Eusebio Francisco Kino came to the San Pedro in 1692 to minister to his flock. And when the depredations of some Apache bands became unbearable, a few decades later, Spanish soldiers picked a site a stone's throw from Coronado's trail and built a *presidio* (garrison) at Quiburi, just west of present-day Fairbank. The crumbling walls of this old fort are still visible, and a belated effort to preserve it as a state or national historic site is now under way.

After marching downriver past today's St. David and Benson, the expedition left the river and "went to the right" to the foothills of the Winchester Mountains. This turn either took them up the Tres Alamos wash or through Texas Canyon along the course Interstate Highway 10 follows today. Here we encounter the first gap in the itinerary outlined by Dr. Bolton forty years ago. For some unexplained reason, he ignored the existence of the Winchesters and guessed that the trail "went a little east of north through the Galiuro range."

From our investigation of this terrain, we consider it more likely that Coronado followed one of two old Indian trails when he reached the headwaters of the Tres Alamos at Allen Flat. The route we favor is a gap through the Winchesters about three miles west of Redrock Canyon. The second prospect is a trail beginning near Hooker Butte in the Sulphur Spring Valley and winding up to a pass between the Galiuro and Winchester mountains

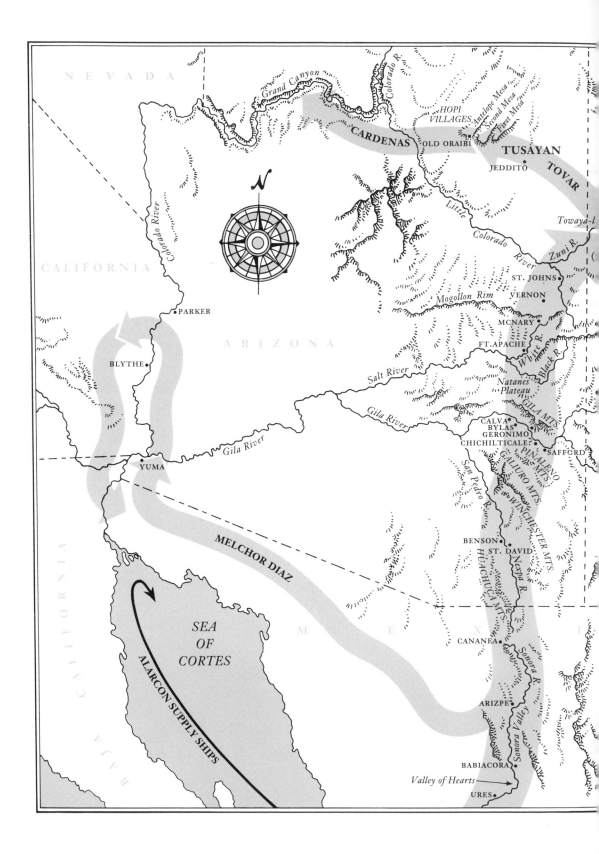

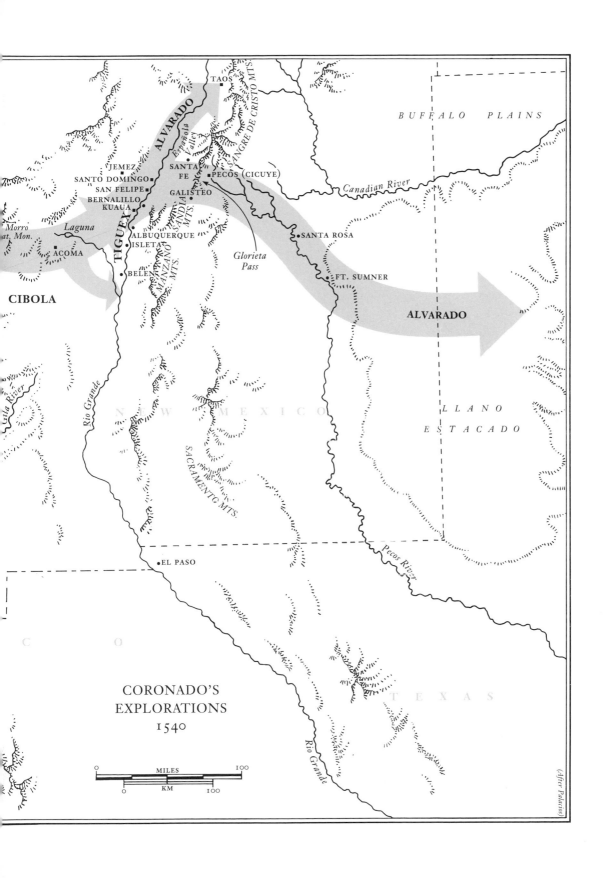

BUFFALO PLAINS

TAOS

ALVARADO

Española Valley

SANGRE DE CRISTO MTS.

JEMEZ

SANTO DOMINGO

SAN FELIPE

BERNALILLO

KUAUA

SANTA FE

GALISTEO

PECOS (CICUYE)

Canadian River

Morro Nat. Mon.

Laguna

TIGUEX

SANDIA MTS.

ALBUQUERQUE

ISLETA

ACOMA

BELEN

MANZANO MTS.

Glorieta Pass

SANTA ROSA

FT. SUMNER

ALVARADO

CIBOLA

Gila River

Rio Grande

N E W   M E X I C O

SACRAMENTO MTS.

L L A N O
E S T A C A D O

EL PASO

Pecos River

C   O

T E X A S

Rio Grande

CORONADO'S
EXPLORATIONS
1540

MILES

0   100

KM

0   100

(After Palacios)

just north of Rockhouse Canyon. Both contain Indian artifacts: Either could be the shortcut that Indian traders used before Coronado came along.

Coronado's destination beyond the pass in the Winchesters was a ruin at "the foot of the cordillera" called the Chichilticale by local Indians. The exact

Arizona: Old trail in a pass of the Winchester Mountains

location of this landmark is a mystery. Its eroding walls were last seen and described as ". . . perfectly filled with stone and mortar . . ." by Captain Juan de Anza in 1775; but by the time scientists began to search for it, in this century, erosion had obliterated its foundations.

The dean of southwestern archaeologists, Dr. Emil W. Haury, of the University of Arizona, has been involved in the search for the Chichilticale for sixty years. He walked over the ground with Dr. Bolton in 1940 and believes it will ultimately be identified by men and women of his profession somewhere near the 76 Ranch, in the foothills of the western flank of the Pinaleno Mountains. At eighty, Dr. Haury is still excited by the riddle of the Red House. When Chichilticale is located, he says, it will enrich science and surely become a premier historic place in our national park system.

Another geography puzzle concerns the location of the nearby Chichilticale Pass, described by Juan Jaramillo. It was at this notch that the Europeans would have had their first glimpse of the region they called the *Despoblado*. It is likely the Chichilticale Pass was part of the nineteenth-century military trail to Fort Grant, which ascended the canyon between Cedar Mountain and Cedar Springs Butte. But, again, Spanish or Indian artifacts should someday provide solid proof of the exact position of this pass in the Pinalenos.

☾ IN THE DESPOBLADO

To vary our past tribulations, we found no grass during the first days and encountered more dangerous passages than we had previously experienced. The horses were so exhausted they could not endure it, and, in this last desert, we lost more than previously. The way is very bad for at least thirty leagues or more through impassable mountains. But, when we had covered these thirty leagues, we found fresh rivers and grass like that of Castile.
—CORONADO TO MENDOZA

When the conquistadores crossed over Chichilticale Pass and rode downhill toward the Gila River, they surely cast fearful glances at the abutments of the Gila Mountains. How could their horses climb these barriers or surmount the near-vertical escarpment that loomed beyond them?

With Cárdenas and fifteen horsemen sprinting ahead, the company waded the Gila somewhere between Gerónimo and Bylas and tackled the terrain that would be the most difficult of their entire trip. For unexplained reasons, Dr. Bolton presumed that from Bylas the trail turned due west for twenty-five miles to present-day San Carlos and "swung around the west end of the Gila range." This is a dubious assumption. Such a detour would have wasted a full week. Moreover, there is ample evidence that the Spaniards followed an existing Indian pathway that turned north at Calva up a steep, ridge-hugging trail that is used today by Apache cowboys to bring their livestock down to the Calva railhead. This very trail served as a key segment of the north–south military road General Crook's cavalry traveled between Fort Apache and Fort

Thomas. So it is logical to assume that General Crook's Apache scouts showed him this beeline route when he set up his system of cavalry posts in the 1870s.

Beyond the Gila range, the explorers found themselves on a treeless grassland that resembles the savannas of East Africa. This tableland extends from the Gila range to the jutting ledges of the Nantack Ridge. Coronado surely had the Nantack in mind when he reported to Mendoza that he and his men faced "impassable" mountains. This promontory appears impenetrable, but there is a "crack" that Indian runners quite certainly found and used as a stairway to the Natanes Plateau.

This stairway, which ascends the narrow canyon of the North Fork of Ash Creek, is undoubtedly the rocky pitch that caused Coronado to report that many of the horses were "so exhausted they could not endure it."

Yet once this ridge was surmounted, the worst was over. The Sonoran Desert was behind them. They were in a forest of pine trees. The nights were cool, and there was a lush carpet of pine needles for their horses to walk on. Shortly they would encounter ". . . fresh rivers and grass like that of Castile."

The Indian trail now led straight toward the landmark Black River Crossing, where a cool stream and abundant grass offered respite for the travelers and their mounts. This mountain paradise must have afforded two or three days of rest and relaxation: There was bathing, the blacksmiths replaced lost horseshoes, and rainbow trout probably supplemented the dwindling rations of the conquistadores.

The route from the Black River to the White River took the party through an unusual forest of huge alligator-bark juniper trees into the open country of Bonita Prairie, where a gap in the chronicles presents another puzzle. Did the 1540 trail cross this large meadow and descend Seven Mile Canyon to a White River crossing just below Fort Apache? Or did it turn to the northwest and descend to Canyon Day through a break in the black rim south of that community? We believe petroglyphs and other Indian markings (drawn by Indian runners waiting for the river to subside) suggest the latter as the most promising site of Coronado's path.

The reports tell us that the White River was in flood and that the Spaniards had to build crude rafts to transport their armor across the stream. Unfortunately, however, there are no clues that help identify the exact location of that impromptu ferry.

It was now late June. The travelers were in the largest ponderosa pine forest on the continent, and the rest of the journey to the Seven Cities would

New Mexico: Zuni Pueblo, ca. 1900

not be strenuous. Two things were on their minds at this stage of their trip: the prospect that another Inca empire was at hand and hunger that told them their food was almost exhausted. This latter preoccupation has always puzzled me. Why, in a region rich in fish and wildlife, did these Spaniards not pause to hunt or fish? Gold fever is a malady that often strips men of their common sense.

There are two possible routes north from the White River crossing to the "barranca," now named Post Office Canyon. One would have clung to the "bench" on the west side of the North Fork where the main highway to Pinetop now runs. A second, more direct trail would have gone up Bear Canyon to a notch just south of Post Office Canyon. After detouring to the west around the barranca, the ancient Indian walkway probably veered northeast to the vicinity of McNary and then paralleled the present dirt road that runs on the roof of the Mogollon Rim from McNary to Vernon.

A bivouac at a spring, most likely near Lake Mountain, brought the horsemen to a site that has a place in history as "the Camp of Death." Here one soldier and several Indian allies perished after eating a wild plant. This succulent root (*Cicuta douglassi*) inflicted illness and death on later travelers and acquired the sinister appellation "water hemlock."

☾ THE SPRINT TO ZUNI

From the Camp of Death, the path descended into open, rolling country, where the Europeans first saw the mesas and long vistas of the Colorado Plateau. There were volcanic knolls and cones, and scouts could ride to their summits and survey natural landmarks a hundred miles away.

Towaya' lane, the sacred Corn Mountain of the Zuni Indians, is visible from some of these lookouts. So it is logical to assume that the old Indian trail followed spring-fed creeks on a direct line toward Cíbola. Such a path would have taken them to the Malpais Spring, down the Big Hollow three miles west of St. Johns, and on to a camp where this arroyo intersects the Little Colorado River.

The level of excitement rose as they reached this "Red River." There the trekkers caught fish "like those in Spain" and encountered "the first Indians in that land." The Spaniards and their faithful historian assumed the natives were scouts sent to keep an eye on the intruders. In his report to the viceroy, Coronado remarked that the scouts ". . . lighted their fires from point to point . . ." to warn the Cíbolans of his approach.

Zuni Indians in our day have a different explanation of these events. This, they point out, was the exact time of year when Zuni religious leaders conduct a pilgrimage to a paramount Zuni shrine a few miles downstream. These natives, they tell us, were priests, not warriors. And the signal fires Coronado observed were a customary message to those at home indicating the sacred rites had been performed—and the gods, once again, had been propitiated.

Be that as it may, a two-day march up the Zuni River brought the hungry army to the outskirts of the land of Cíbola. There the cautious Coronado sent Cárdenas ahead to forestall a surprise attack. Cárdenas pitched a camp in a

New Mexico: Hawikuh ruin and grassy meadow where the Spanish first glimpsed the "Golden City"

colorful oxbow of the Zuni River near today's boundary between the states of Arizona and New Mexico. This "Bad Pass" has a place in history because it was the scene of a midnight ambush that produced the first military skirmish between Indians and Europeans in the American West.

The next morning, the advance guard pushed beyond Bad Pass onto an open meadow, and a moment of truth was at hand. This was a day they would all remember. Now they would feast their eyes on the glistening "golden city" Fray Marcos supposedly had studied in wonderment a year earlier. A fever surely raced through the minds of Coronado and his men as they rode onto the grassy plain. Would the Inca daydreams they had nurtured be fulfilled? "Is this the place?" the anxious commander must have asked the friar.

At a distance, the appearance of this multistoried mud structure was not reassuring. On the brow of a low hill, it seemed "all crumpled together." There were no signs of temples or battlements or decorated portals. But this was no time for speculation. A battle order was issued. The mettle of Coronado's little "army" would finally be tested.

The military accoutrements lugged all the way from Spain were now the focus of attention. Those who had horse armor equipped their steeds; men donned their personal armor; lances and swords were unsheathed; and foot soldiers unloaded their crossbows and muskets and checked the mechanisms of these emblems of European firepower. Once the captains reported they were ready, Coronado led his troop to a battle line Zuni defenders had drawn by spreading sacred cornmeal on the ground outside the wall of their city.

Coronado offered gifts and made conciliatory gestures. But his acts were interpreted as a sign of timidity, and the Indians launched an attack that brought them "almost to the heels of our horses to fire their arrows" (as Coronado wrote later in admiration). The captain general then sounded the traditional war cry, *Santiago-y-a-ellos* (For St. James and at them!). The Battle of Hawikuh had begun.

The uneven contest raged furiously for maybe an hour. The Cíbolans resisted from the terraces of their pueblo until their supplies of arrows and rocks ran out. Then they fled to the hills. No Spaniards were slain, and there were only a few Zuni casualties. But Coronado, the prime target of the Zuni missiles in his plumed helmet, was knocked senseless by well-aimed rocks.

The Battle of Hawikuh, on July 7, 1540, was the first formal military encounter between Europeans and natives in what is now the United States. The
Zunis stood their ground and used their crude weapons with determination
and skill. The fury of this unequal contest—and Coronado's close call with
death—were described vividly by Castañeda:

> *The Spaniards then attacked the village, which was taken*
> *with not a little difficulty, since they held the narrow and*
> *crooked entrance. During the attack they knocked the gen-*
> *eral down with a large stone, and would have killed him*
> *but for Don García López de Cárdenas and Hernando de*
> *Alvarado, who threw themselves above him and drew him*
> *away, receiving the blows of the stones, which were not few.*

Inside the walls of Hawikuh, the hungry soldiers found storehouses filled
with maize and beans, which they ". . . prized more than gold or silver." But
there were no traces of the ornaments and gems foretold by Fray Marcos.
Coronado later described the total treasure trove yielded by the Seven Cities
as ". . . two points of emerald and some little broken stones, rather poor,
which approach the color of garnet."

Marcos, it was plain, had concocted a report a year earlier based on rumors,
not facts. He had never seen the land of Cíbola; the seven golden cities that
he depicted as having riches that compared with those described by Marco Polo
were castles in the air conjured up by an imagination running out of control.

When Coronado regained consciousness, he had to face both the effects
of his concussion and a psychological trauma that tested the resilience of his
character. Unless a surprise lurked somewhere, his expedition was a failure, a
journey to nowhere. The dispatch he sent to Mendoza was blunt and matter-
of-fact: ". . . everything," he wrote, "was the reverse" of what Fray Marcos
had said.

It is obvious that Don Francisco's gold fever was quenched at Cíbola.
Fortunately for history, it is equally clear that he was a determined explorer
who would swallow his disappointment and conduct a wide-ranging quest
for information about this new land before retracing his steps to New Spain.

The Great Season of Exploration: 1540

. . . I have decided to send men throughout all the surrounding regions in order to find out if there is anything worth while; to suffer every hardship rather than abandon this enterprise.

—LETTER FROM CORONADO
TO VICEROY MENDOZA,
AUGUST 3, 1540

THE MOST VIVID AND INTERESTING of the Coronado documents is the report Don Francisco sent to Viceroy Mendoza soon after his "new Peru" dreams were shattered at Hawikuh. It reveals, unmistakably, the temper of the man Mendoza had picked to be his "Cortés." It also tells us about Coronado's state of mind in the late summer of 1540.

The self-portrait this letter draws reveals an honest man bent on relaying accurate information to his superior. It also explains why Castañeda once described Don Francisco as a "beloved leader." Coronado was generous: He bestowed praise on his lieutenants, and he demonstrated concern for the welfare of the Negroes and Indians who served as his support troops.

Don Francisco also comes across as a tolerant, humane leader. He reported that Fray Marcos "has not told the truth in a single thing that he said," but he did not use harsh language or try to make a scapegoat of the provincial. And it is obvious that Coronado agreed with—and was making a serious effort to enforce—the viceroy's order that the natives be treated with respect.

Some authors have pictured Don Francisco as a gold-hungry optimist who sent out side expeditions from Hawikuh with the expectation that an Eldorado would be found. There is little that supports this interpretation. The letter to Mendoza was permeated with pessimism: The captain general saw no hope of "getting gold or silver," and his assumption that these farmer Indians had never developed an interest in gathering precious metals was both sober and sensible.

It is clear that Hernando de Alvarado, and perhaps other captains as well, was still infected with gold fever, but nothing suggests Coronado ever allowed his hopes to soar after the myths of Fray Marcos were shattered at Hawikuh. His letter was filled with mundane facts about Zuni culture, and nothing in it implied that Coronado believed this austere region sheltered hidden valleys where rich Indians held sway.

A new phase of his expedition was unfolding as Don Francisco gave his report to the express riders on August 3, 1540. Accompanied by Zuni guides, Captain Tovar had been dispatched earlier with a small scouting party to the Hopi villages to check out this "kingdom." And other decisions were made in short order to send Melchor Díaz back to Sonora to organize a search for Alarcán's supply ships at the South Sea, to post Cárdenas to investigate the "great river" in the west, and to command young Alvarado to lead a detachment of mounted men to explore the land of the other Pueblo Indians in the east.

By making these decisions, the captain general set the stage for a great surge of inland exploration: In less than six months, Coronado's outriders verified the vastness of western North America by carrying the Spanish flag to western Sonora, to California, to Arizona's Grand Canyon, to the middle section of the Rio Grande Valley, and to the buffalo plains near the Texas Panhandle. No explorers of any later century covered as much ground—or made as many sightings of undiscovered lands—as did Coronado's captains in the final months of 1540.

Although Tovar, Cárdenas, Melchor Díaz, and Alvarado found no gold, their feats secured a prominent niche in New World history for the Coronado expedition. Let us retrace the journeys of these long riders as they won an array of geographical consolation prizes for their luckless commander.

☾ TOVAR TO TUSAYAN

Don Pedro's trip to the Hopi villages (called the province of Tusayan by Fray Marcos) was the shortest and least venturesome of those forays. Its main purpose, of course, was to determine if the Hopi towns had riches not possessed by the cities of Cíbola.

There was undoubtedly a well-beaten path between these communities of cousins. The chronicles tell us the Hopis came to the Zuni country on a regular basis to harvest salt at a saline pool south of Hawikuh. Thus, it is a good guess that the trail Tovar took went by Navajo Springs and then on a direct line to the eastern entrance of the Jeddito Valley.

The confrontation at Antelope Mesa was a reenactment of the encounter at Hawikuh. Tovar made demands, the Hopis drew a line with sacred cornmeal on the earth, there was a hostile act by a Hopi warrior, the Santiago war cry was given, and Spanish swords prevailed over Indian clubs and arrows. Once the Hopi warriors were routed, "very intelligent" Hopi elders appeared bearing gifts and making amicable gestures.

Tovar next traveled to villages at the base of the other Hopi mesas. There similar obeisances were performed. It is also likely that Tovar and some of his men clambered up the Third Mesa to inspect the village now known as Old Oraibi. This Pueblo vies with Acoma as the oldest continuously inhabited town in the United States, but obviously Tovar had no way of knowing he was in the presence of a historic curiosity.

Castañeda tells us that Tovar's company returned in good order with news that there was a "great river" west of Tusayan that should be investigated. The existence of this mystery prompted Coronado to dispatch a larger force, under Cárdenas, to locate the river and determine whether it could be followed downstream to the South Sea.

CÁRDENAS TO THE GRAND CANYON

The width of the continent at this latitude was unknown—and would still be a mystery to Spaniards as late as 1776, when Father Escalante led a search mission from Santa Fe looking for an overland trail to California—but Coronado must have assumed that his *maestro de campo* might follow this river to its mouth in the eighty days he allotted for his reconnaissance.

The *maestro* retraced Tovar's route to Tusayan, acquired some Indian guides, and turned west on a trail the Hopis apparently used to travel to Havasupai Canyon. This brought his party to the South Rim of the Grand Canyon, probably in the vicinity of Grand View Point. Here was a panoramic view of a scenic chasm—and beyond it, "lying open toward the north," the Spaniards could see on the horizon the heartland of the Colorado Plateau, which, in our day, contains the heaviest concentration of national parks in the United States.

At first the discoverers' eyes were deceived by the scale of the abyss. In its bed a mile below, to them the great river looked "like a brook" measuring "six feet across," even though their Hopi guides told them that the river was half a league wide. In an effort to ascertain its dimensions, Cárdenas sent three of his "lightest and most agile men," under Pablo de Melgosa, to climb down to the river. Those pioneer rock climbers spent a full day inching along a ridge and got "about a third of the way down" before they had to turn back. The depth of the barrier verified, Cárdenas decided to saddle up and ride west along the South Rim.

Now a different natural barrier reared its head. The Hopi said there was so little water along the South Rim "for three or four days" that it was their practice when they crossed this region to take along women ". . . loaded with water in gourds, and bury the gourds of water along the way, to use when they return." The Hopi also imparted the information that their runners needed less water because ". . . they travel in one day what it takes us two days to accomplish." (This report should not evoke skepticism in our day, for at the Olympic Games in 1912 an "untrained" Hopi Indian, Lewis Tewanema, ran the 10,000-meter race in a time that was not surpassed by a U.S. runner for more than half a century.)

Cárdenas apparently listened to his Hopi friends, for he soon abandoned his search and returned to Hawikuh. The "written account of what they had seen," presented to Coronado, has vanished. If it ever turns up, the world will know the reaction of Europe's first "tourists" to the stupendous natural wonder called the Grand Canyon of the Colorado.

☾ MELCHOR DÍAZ DISCOVERS CALIFORNIA

One captain, Melchor Díaz, stands out in the Coronado crowd. Díaz was not a well-born gentleman adventurer who sought his fortune on the expedition to the Seven Cities. He was a Spanish frontiersman who was thrown into the breach by superiors who had tested his mettle and needed his wilderness skills.

In 1540, Melchor Díaz knew more about northern natives and Indian trails than any other Spaniard in the New World. He was, if we read between the lines of the Coronado chronicles, a natural leader who was as fearless as he was tireless. One companion described him as a "beloved leader" who "merited the position he held." It was Díaz, remember, who welcomed Cabeza de Vaca and his castaways back to civilization in 1536 when he was the *alcalde* of Culiacán. And Díaz was the scout the cautious Viceroy Mendoza picked to make a fast trip into Arizona's wilderness in the fall of 1539 to resolve his lingering doubts about Fray Marcos's report.

Melchor Díaz carried out more far-ranging assignments in 1540 than any other conquistador. He exemplified Spanish energy and fortitude: He rode more miles, saw more unexplored country, took more risks, and blazed more trails than any other captain who took part in this entrada.

Melchor Díaz was our first frontiersman. He started the last year of his life in the snows of Chichilticale, where he was waiting for winter to break so he could ride south and present his report to the viceroy. In late March, as we have seen, Díaz intercepted Coronado and his plodding army at Chiametla. There, on command, he whirled about and served as the principal outrider of the Coronado expedition.

Melchor Díaz received his final orders from Don Francisco soon after the battle of Hawikuh. He was told to return to the Sonora Valley and tell Captain Arellano to move the main force to Cíbola. Díaz was also instructed to organize a remnant group of soldiers into a settlement (San Gerónimo) that could serve as a supply depot for the forces in the north. That done, he was ordered to travel west into an unexplored desert, find the flotilla of Alarcón —and bring the supplies from his ships back to the new base of operations in Sonora.

The location of the path Díaz followed to the Colorado River is another Coronado trail puzzle. Herbert Bolton and his University of California colleague Carl Sauer concluded he probably followed an Indian trail up the Altar Valley to Sonoita and then made the first European crossing of a stark stretch

Arizona: Awatovi ruins and Jeddito Valley on the Hopi Reservation

of the Sonoran Desert—known in the nineteenth century as the Camino del Diablo (the Devil's Highway)—along the international border to the Yuma area. Others believe Díaz came to Yuma by following the seacoast. There is little evidence to support either thesis.

In any event, the chronicles tell us this faithful scout negotiated a passage to the Colorado River and found a message Alarcón had buried in a tree two months earlier, before he sailed back to Mexico. He then decided to head upstream and see if that big river held any important secrets.

There is a consensus that Díaz probably pushed upriver fifty leagues, crossed the Colorado (thus becoming the first European to set foot on what is now California soil), and traversed an area of sand dunes north of Blythe in the region where California's Mohave Mountains are situated. He sustained a mortal groin wound when he accidentally ran into the butt of a lance he had thrown. We know, too, that Captain Díaz was carried for a few days on a litter before he died and was buried "in a wild place."

Heroic is the word to describe the life of Melchor Díaz. He was our first "mountain man." His deeds as an American explorer have never been excelled.

Alvarado's New Mexico Entrada

Vázquez de Coronado tapped another of his favorites, Hernando de Alvarado, to lead the last scouting party. Don Hernando was one of the stalwarts who fought alongside the captain general at Hawikuh and carried him to safety when he was wounded. He was assigned twenty men and sent to explore in the east for eighty days.

The appearance of a peace mission from one of the eastern pueblos emboldened Don Francisco to send such a tiny force into this region of strong towns. News of the mounted invaders had spread via the "moccasin telegraph," and two emissaries had walked three hundred miles from Cicuye (Pecos) to meet the strangers and see the huge animals they rode. The two "captains" —nicknamed Cacique (Governor) and Bigotes (Whiskers) by the Spaniards —announced they had come "to offer themselves as friends." They told Coronado about the many villages along a great river in the east and the immense herds of wild cattle that roamed on plains beyond their homes.

The captain general liked Bigotes. He described him as ". . . a tall young man, well built and robust in appearance," and when the gregarious Whiskers offered himself as an escort/intermediary, Coronado eagerly assented.

With Bigotes leading the way, from Hawikuh Alvarado marched in a direct line south of the Zuni Valley to the Sky City of Acoma. The first leg of Alvarado's journey took him through what today are some of the finest unspoiled Coronadoscapes on the 1540 trail. Here is the heartland of Haniel Long's piñon country: As far as the eye can see on both slopes of the Continental Divide, dwarfed piñon, juniper, and cedar trees are intermixed in forest patterns that exemplify this special geographical region of the Southwest.

Today one can see some of these landscapes by sauntering along Route 17 south of Grants on a little-known road that should be named the Coronado Scenic Parkway. Here one sees the same natural features—the unusual forests, the great meadows, the "frozen" river of lava, Ventana Natural Arch on the edge of the Cebollita Mesa, and the distant, serrated skyline of the Datil Range—which the Spanish explorers saw four and a half centuries ago.

The old path of the Indian runners may have snaked through these lava badlands, but I am convinced that the Spaniards probably skirted to the south around this barrier to protect the hooves of their horses. The precise location of this road to Acoma is unknown, but it undoubtedly ascended the Cebollita Mesa and descended Acoma Canyon to the Enchanted Mesa and the fortress city itself.

Alvarado was probably uneasy as his party approached the abutments of Acoma. Bigotes surely had warned him that their rocky perch had instilled in these natives a rebellious independence that made them the combative eagles of puebloland. He regarded this natural fort as "one of the strongest ever seen," and a companion observed that had these Indians ". . . remained on their rock . . . we would not have been able to disturb them in the least."

Acoma still evokes wonder. Save for a regrettable roadway blasted up one of its walls, this stronghold enjoys the same solitary splendor it knew that September afternoon in 1540. It is, arguably, the most dramatic historic site anywhere in the United States.

At Acoma, Bigotes produced the first of the outdoor peace pageants that made Alvarado's scouting expedition such a success. We do not know what counsel he gave the elders—or how he quieted the voices of young warriors who were expert at ambushing intruders—but we do know Whiskers worked his mediation magic and the natives "came down peacefully." There was a gift-exchange ceremony, and some of the Spaniards were taken up the "ladder trail" to visit the village in the sky.

From Acoma, Whiskers guided the Spaniards north to a lake (where the Laguna Indians later settled) and then eastward to a camp on the Rio Grande near present-day Isleta, where the Manzano Mountains form a blue backdrop east of the river. Bigotes then went upstream alone, "with a cross," to reason with the headmen of the twelve Tigua villages along the west bank of the river. The Spaniards called this area the Province of Tigüex. The next day, Bigotes appeared leading a welcoming committee ". . . in good order . . . of chieftains and people. They marched around our tent, playing a flute and with an old man for spokesman," Don Hernando wrote, and "came inside the tent and presented me with food, cotton cloth, and skins which they had."

It was harvest time, and the Indians were in their fields as the Spanish contingent rode by the Tigua towns. Alvarado was impressed by this "broad valley planted with fields of maize and dotted with cottonwood groves." Noting the "great abundance" of maize, beans, melons, and turkeys, he commented that "the natives seem to be good people, more devoted to agriculture than war."

Time and erosion have obliterated most of the Tigua villages, but the state of New Mexico saved a remnant of this heritage in the 1920s when it created the Coronado State Monument, north of Bernalillo, to preserve the Kuaua ruins. Archaeologists have identified the sites of some of the other Tigua towns, one of which is within the Albuquerque city limits. Some experts believe this ruin is the remains of Alcanfor, the pueblo where Coronado maintained his headquarters for a year and a half. If they are correct, that site should contain one of the richest troves of Coronado artifacts in the Southwest.

Their march upriver took the discoverers across what today is the most heavily urbanized area traversed by the conquistadores. Some communities on the west bank of the Rio Grande from Isleta north to Bernalillo literally sit on top of a chapter of American history. Today's residents of metropolitan Albuquerque share the ambience Coronado experienced at Tigüex: The

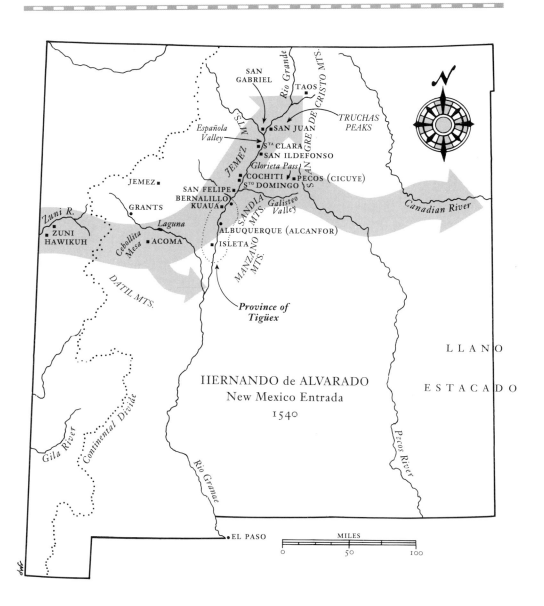

HERNANDO de ALVARADO
New Mexico Entrada
1540

great river has kept its channel and its groves of cottonwood trees—and the
Sandia Mountains still brood over the scene in the eloquent light of changing
seasons and skies.

North of Tigüex country, Bigotes produced yet another of his ceremonies
of friendship. Alvarado does not inform us whether there was more flute
music, but he wrote to Coronado that ". . . the Indians from the surrounding

provinces came to offer me peace." The young Pecos leader undoubtedly used the moccasin telegraph to summon elders from all of the northern pueblos to this auspicious gathering.

Alvarado's terse report contains few details about his upriver route, but since we know his trek took place in late August, when the river was low, it is

New Mexico: Acoma from balcony of church of San Esteban

likely he and his horsemen forded the stream several times as they inspected the middle pueblos of Santo Domingo, San Felipe, and Cochiti. And beyond White Rock Canyon they emerged into the Española Valley and found themselves between two beautiful *sierras:* the Jemez to the west and to the east what the later Spaniards would call the Sangre de Cristo (Blood of Christ) Mountains. It is a good surmise these landscapes reminded some soldiers of familiar scenes in the cordilleras of central Spain. The logical route should have taken them by the pueblos of San Ildefonso, Santa Clara, San Juan, and San Gabriel as they pushed on to the black-rock gorge of the Rio Grande, where the Truchas Peaks beckoned on their right as they approached the Taos Pueblo in its majestic mountain setting.

The mountain Indians of Taos wore clothes of deerskin and buffalo hides, and their thriving community had "more inhabitants than any other pueblo in that land." But Bigotes again worked his magic and the Taoseños (who could have easily overwhelmed the small Spanish force) welcomed the visitors and offered them "apartments" within their pueblo. Don Hernando diplomatically declined, even though it was October and it was colder "in the sierras."

Captain Alvarado next retraced his path to Tigüex, where he sent riders
with a map and a messenger urging Coronado to establish winter quarters in
the warmer climate along the Rio Grande. Don Hernando next turned eastward to learn about "the cows" and the great plain where they wandered.

New Mexico: Taos Pueblo

Bigotes now led his friends on a familiar homeward path up the Galisteo Valley,
past several Tano towns, through Lamy Canyon, and over Glorieta Pass to the
Pecos Pueblo. A musical salute welcomed the party as it was ushered inside
the walls of the fortress. The Spaniards were impressed by these Indians. Their
town was ". . . larger than any of the others and very strong. Its houses are
four and five storeys high, some of them being very fine. It has eight large

patios, each with its corridor. These people neither plant cotton nor raise turkeys, because it is . . . close to the plains where the cattle roam."

The narrow valley occupied by the Pecos Indians is drenched in history. In 1540—and for more than three centuries thereafter—the Pecos Pueblo

New Mexico: The ruins of Kuaua Pueblo (Coronado State Monument)

sat astride a natural passageway used by Indian and non-Indian travelers who wanted to move between the Rio Grande Valley and the buffalo plains. This imposing pueblo and the adjacent massive church erected by Spanish missionaries were renowned landmarks until the last wagons rolled by on the Santa Fe Trail.

It is fitting that this site is today one of the most fascinating and best-interpreted monuments maintained by the National Park Service. Here one can absorb a millennial story of human striving that begins with antiquity and ends when the first railroad engines surmounted Glorieta Pass in 1880.

New Mexico: "Tent Rocks," Cochiti Pueblo

Bigotes assigned two "captive" Plains Indians to guide Alvarado from Pecos into the buffalo country. One was Sopete, a Quivira Indian; the other was a wily native from eastern Kansas whom the Spaniards dubbed "the Turk."

The accounts are sketchy, so it is difficult to determine the route the Spaniards took or how far east they went on this inaugural European buffalo hunt. Dr. Bolton assumed they traveled down the Pecos River "some distance," then cut due north and followed the Canadian River almost to the Texas Panhandle. Bolton's assumption that these explorers did not climb onto the great mesa called the Llano Estacado is puzzling, as Alvarado's description of a plain "as level as the sea" does not fit the rolling country along the Canadian River.

In any event, we have a good description of the first Old World encounter with the most massive aggregation of large animals in the world. Wildlife experts tell us that more than sixty million bison ranged over the middle section of North America in the sixteenth century, so Alvarado's troops saw these animals when they were at or near their prime.

The Spaniards were astounded by that wild kingdom and its profusion of "monstrous beasts." "There is such a quantity of them," one witness wrote, "that I do not know what to compare them with, except with the fish of the sea. . . . There were so many that many times when we . . . wanted to go through to the other side of them, we were not able to, because the country was covered with them." The brave bulls had "wicked horns" and killed several horses before Alvarado's men learned that the pike was "the best weapon to use against them, and the musket for use when this misses."

However, the buffalo were overshadowed when the Turk began talking about a rich land called Quivira *más allá* (farther on), which emerged (as eager Spaniards embellished his words) as a country that had ". . . gold, silver and fabrics . . . and abundance in everything."

It is astonishing that Don Hernando de Alvarado (who apparently learned little during the Seven Cities fiasco) was taken in by the Turk's tale or by his assertion that Bigotes had a "golden bracelet" he had secured from the rich Indians of Quivira. But it is obvious Don Hernando's gold fever was rekindled, and a turning point for the expedition was at hand when he raced back to Pecos to force Bigotes to produce the bracelet and provide details about the gilded civilization in the east.

New Mexico: Ancient stairway to Acoma Pueblo

The Bad Winter on the Rio Grande

. . . the strangers [Spaniards] did not respect the peace they had made, which afterward proved a great misfortune.
—CASTAÑEDA

APART FROM HIS FAILURE to find nonexistent cities of gold, as September's frost forced him to think about winter survival Coronado could review the accomplishments of his *entrada* with pride. With a tiny complement of eighty men he had brought a vast swath of *tierra incógnita* (unknown land) under Spanish dominion. His captains had performed their assignments with skill and dispatch. And he had avoided the use of force—and thus carried out the king's treat-the-natives-with-kindness policy—except on those occasions when hostile Indians had forced him to take military action.

Summer's successes, however, were followed by blunders that led to a destructive, unnecessary Indian war in the land of the Tigua Indians along the Rio Grande. The pressures that provoked the Tigüex War would have been lessened had Don Francisco ordered Arellano and the main force to remain in Sonora in the region the Zuni Indians called "the land of everlasting summer."

From any point of view, Coronado's decision to move the force north was a blunder. He did not need additional soldiers and was surely aware that his troops, and particularly their thin-blooded Indian allies, were not prepared for the rigors of high-country weather. This movement quadrupled pressures on the limited resources of the Pueblo Indians and put the Spaniards in a posture where they would have faced starvation—or subsisted on horse meat —had it not been the practice of the thrifty Pueblo farmers to lay up surplus supplies of maize.

The general's second Tigüex blunder was his failure to understand that he needed a wise Indian mediator to help him communicate with his new hosts and reduce the tensions that would inevitably arise. With an astute native always at his elbow, Hernán Cortés knew how to placate Indian concerns before they became inflamed. It is one of the sorrows of his saga that Vázquez de Coronado did not have a Cortesian touch with Indians.

Castañeda made the incisive observation that the winter war came about because the Spaniards ". . . did not respect the peace they had made." Worse yet, they did not respect the peacemaker—Bigotes—who had been the architect of their summer amity. A shadow of irony lies over this sad episode because the masterful young mediator from Pecos—who might have forestalled the escalations that produced the war—sat in chains in Coronado's headquarters, falsely accused of deceiving those he had befriended.

Bigotes must have liked the Spaniards, for his work as a volunteer mediator between the strangers and his Pueblo brothers was a striking success. The young chief's honesty and friendship were affirmed at every town Alvarado visited in the Rio Grande Valley. Had Bigotes been treacherous, it would have been easy for him to arrange an ambush at one of the larger villages and wipe out Alvarado and his twenty scouts.

After Bigotes repeatedly demonstrated his loyalty and friendship, it confounds us that Alvarado suddenly turned on him and believed the Turk's incredible tale that Bigotes was concealing a "golden bracelet" he had acquired somewhere in Quivira. Alvarado's reaction was both arrogant and obtuse. The Indians knew nothing about gold. Alvarado's betrayal of his friend was so unjust, one wonders why Coronado was taken in by his misjudgments.

In any event, the stage was set for a conflict at Tigüex when the captain general moved his headquarters from Hawikuh to the Rio Grande Valley. Cárdenas, sent ahead to prepare quarters, decided the Indians should vacate one of their pueblos—and in due course the southernmost of the twelve Tigüex towns, Alcanfor, was established as the new base of operations.

When Arellano and his shivering army arrived at Hawikuh, in late November, Coronado ordered them to recuperate for twenty days and then set out with a small party for the Rio Grande. After a stopover at Acoma, the general detoured south to inspect the pueblos of the Piros Indians, at Tutahaco, near today's Belen.

Captain Arellano, who moved his ragtag army east in early December, deserves high marks for his leadership. The fact that he got his large herd of livestock and ill-prepared Indian allies across the White Mountains in November with few casualties is a tribute to his generalship, as well as an indication that there was a spell of balmy weather in Arizona's mountain country that fall. One can picture his ill-clad men huddling around big bonfires and nursing flames under overhanging cliffs while they waited for the late-rising sun to make another day on the trail endurable.

On his way to Tigüex, it was Arellano's lot to be the discoverer of a few patches of virgin country. He was told to take the "direct road" and thus was the first Spaniard to lead soldiers to Acoma by marching up the Zuni Valley, through Guadalupe Pass, and by San Rafael, Grants, and McCartys to the Sky City. Arellano may also have been the first European to inspect the handsome headland now known as El Morro National Monument.

There is no inscription rock in the country that compares with El Morro. Its soft sandstone holds petroglyphs pecked into its surface long centuries ago by aboriginal artists. It contains the oldest signature on our continent: a dagger-drawn message cut by Governor Juan de Oñate in April 1605. And it exhibits an array of messages to the world from Spanish officials, priests, soldiers— and nineteenth-century migrants, prospectors, engineers, and cavalrymen— that makes it a unique outdoor register of Western history.

There is no other gallery of symbols and signatures like this anywhere in the United States. Here, in a lonely dell, is an outdoor chapel that silently celebrates part of the great concourse of human endeavor on our continent. All who pause and ponder the messages on the walls of El Morro absorb an unutterable reverence for life and history.

We do not know whether Arellano's benumbed men camped at El Morro, but we do know that by the time they straggled into Alcanfor the skirmishes that touched off the Tigüex "rebellion" had already occurred.

The conduct of the conquistadores at Tigüex is puzzling because in his four months at Hawikuh, Don Francisco had established a pattern of friendly relations with the Zuni Indians. There were frequent talks, few clashes, and Zuni guides won the respect of their new friends. Yet when the Spaniards reached the Rio Grande, their attitude changed. There were no serious peace talks, no efforts to promote live-and-let-live cooperation. It seems that Coronado and his lieutenants assumed the role of insensitive, hard-nosed conquerors once they arrived at their winter quarters.

Cortés, a master of Indian psychology, knew that arrogance invariably breeds trouble when one is outnumbered. His policy was to use force only as

New Mexico: Manzano Mountains and the Rio Grande Valley

a last resort. If Coronado ever understood this truth, he lost it on the road to the province of Tigüex, for the narratives reveal it was arrogant, demanding conduct that poisoned relations with the Tigua Indians. In recounting the story of the requisitioning of winter clothing, the candid Castañeda tells us that natives were ordered to hand over the cloaks on their backs ". . . without any consideration or respect, and without inquiring about the importance of the person despoiled."

Allowing the Tigüex War to occur was a grievous mistake. Coronado apparently made no real effort to avoid frictions that ended in bloodshed and punitive military action. Had a mediator been used, he might have secured cooperation with the argument: "They will leave us in peace when the snows

New Mexico: Inscription at El Morro by Governor Juan de Oñate, dated 16 April 1605, the oldest European signature-artifact in the U.S.

melt if we let them have what they need." But Don Francisco either felt the Tigua Indians could not be pacified or else he simply failed to control his iron-handed lieutenants.

The cause of the clashes that ensued was simple: The conquistadores were aggressors and the Indian "landlords" responded in kind to their hostile acts. Coronado then escalated the violence by viewing angry Indian acts as an insurrection, which had to be put down by the harsh military measures Spaniards customarily used in Europe.

Events now moved with the certain sweep of a Greek tragedy. Sullen Indians killed Spanish horses, Cárdenas led an all-out assault on the pueblo of Arenal, European arms prevailed over Indian clubs and arrows—and there was a grisly sixteenth-century military denouement when thirty or more Indian warriors were burned at the stake.

Inexorably the bloody business at Arenal turned the ratchet of war to its highest notch: The Spaniards rode about demanding unconditional submission, and the Tigua warriors fled to their strongest pueblo (Moho) to wage a valiant last-ditch fight for their lives. Having destroyed the foundation of trust, Vázquez de Coronado took over and led a destructive winter-long siege that ended with two hundred dead Indians, ten or more slain Spaniards, and twelve Tigüex pueblos burned or abandoned.

The Tigüex War is a dark stain that can never be expunged from the banner of Francisco Vázquez de Coronado. Of all the New World conquistadores (except, perhaps, Hernán Cortés), this general was usually the most humane and generous in his dealings with Indians. When one surveys the overall record of this man from Salamanca, the winter war he waged along the Rio Grande seems like an aberration, like the blind thrashings of a person temporarily deranged.

On the Texas Plains

The memoirs and journals of the Spanish explorers . . .
revealed few expressions of surprise and astonishment
about the nature of the country . . . [on the Great Plains]
the Spaniard . . . found himself in an environment not
unlike that in which he had lived for thirty generations.

In the Plains area lived one animal that came nearer to
dominating the life . . . of a human race than any other
in all the land, if not the world—the buffalo.
—WALTER PRESCOTT WEBB,
The Great Plains

WHEN CORONADO CAME OUT of the mountains and crossed over the Pecos
River, he was entering—and would be the first to extensively explore—a
natural phenomenon that would be both a barrier and an object of awe to
Europeans who later approached its edges. Here was an immense grassland
that covered the central core of the North American continent and extended
from the Rio Grande to Great Slave Lake in northern Canada.

The appearance of foreign cavalrymen on those tablelands foreshadowed
a significant development in the history of the American West. There were no
horses in the New World when the Spaniards arrived, so it stirs our imagination to realize that horses and horsemanship first became a factor in human
affairs in the only comparable geographical area on earth: the steppes of central Asia. The environment of the Kirghiz steppes produced the horses and
masters of military horsemanship (the "primitive" Huns) who overran other
civilizations and transformed warfare in the West. Thus, history's screw made
a sublime twist when on this continent civilized Spaniards revolutionized the
lives of aboriginal folk by introducing a stock of wild horses that gave the
Indians of our steppes an opportunity to mount up and become, almost
overnight, unsurpassed equestrians.

But that development was more than six generations down the road; the
natives Coronado met were earthbound creatures whose lives were controlled
by another noble animal, the American buffalo. A few days east of the Pecos,
Coronado and his companions saw, cropping the luxuriant grasses of the High
Plains, the wildlife wonder of the planet: Grazing in herds ranging from hundreds to as many as several million, these animals constituted the largest aggregation of four-legged creatures on any continent in any period of recorded
history. Coronado described the bison as so omnipresent that during all his
travels that long summer ". . . there was not a single day until my return that
I lost sight of them."

Soon after reaching the "domain of the cows," the Spaniards came upon the buffalo-hide tents of Indians who were living among the buffalo. Called Querechos by the Pecos guides, these nomads had evolved a symbiotic relationship to the bison. Castañeda described their way of life with a precision modern anthropologists might envy: "These Indians subsist . . . entirely on cattle, for they neither plant nor harvest maize. With the skins they build their houses; with the skins they clothe and shoe themselves; from the skins they make ropes and also obtain wool. From the sinews they make thread, with which they sew their clothing and likewise their tents. From the bones they shape awls, and the dung they use for firewood, since there is no other fuel in all that land. The bladders serve as jugs and drinking vessels. They sustain themselves on the flesh of the animals, eating it slightly roasted…and sometimes uncooked . . . they eat raw fat without warming it, and drink the blood just as it comes from the cattle. . . . They have no other food."

Along with their primitive habits, those buffalo Indians had ". . . gentle . . . intelligent" traits. They harnessed large dogs (probably domesticated wolves) to pull their belongings across the prairie, and their skill at skinning buffalo and tanning their hides provided them with products to barter with the Pueblo Indians.

I have often wondered whether one of these animal-conscious Indians requested a ride on a Spanish pony and contemplated how his life might be altered if he possessed a horse. It would take many decades, but Spanish colonies in northern Mexico would later propagate herds of wild horses and transform the buffalo Indians into horse Indians with new skills and an exciting new way of living.

When Plains Indians learned to capture and train Mexican mustangs, the historian W. P. Webb says, this achievement "glorified" the Plains tribes and lifted them ". . . up to an eminence that they could not attain as footmen of the plains." Webb wrote that the horsemanship perfected by American Indians "aroused the wonder and admiration of all who observed it" and generated progress that made the eighteenth century ". . . the golden century of the Plains Indians."

But, again, that adventure lay in the future. In the spring of 1541 the gentle Querecho Indians had pedestrian tasks to perform. It was their lot to instruct their Spanish visitors in buffalo lore—and to guide them onto the great tableland known in our era as the Llano Estacado.

The Llano is almost as large as the state of Indiana, and its flatness was described best by Coronado in a letter to the king: "I traveled," the captain general wrote, ". . . as the guides wished to lead me, until I reached some plains, with no more landmarks than as if we had been swallowed up by the sea, where they strayed about, because there was not a stone nor a bit of rising ground, nor a tree, nor a shrub, nor anything to go by." There, teeming with bison, gray wolves, and pronghorn antelope, was a landscape so flat and confusing that the Spaniards blindly followed the beckonings of the Turk.

Everything, including the grass, contributed to their bewilderment: One Spaniard remembered that ". . . although the grass was short, after it was trampled upon it stood up again as clean and straight as before," and another that ". . . it became necessary to stack up piles of bones and buffalo chips at various distances" so the rear guard would not get lost. It has been impossible for history buffs to plot the course of Coronado's travels in West Texas, for the Llano Estacado conspired to make the Spaniards miscalculate distances and directions.

Fortunately, there are sufficient clues in the chronicles to encourage trail aficionados to argue and speculate about likely pathways. The accounts tell us, for example, that south of the place they met the Querechos, the soldiers contacted a different tribe of natives (the Teyas Indians) at a turning point identified as the "First Barranca." It is also clear that at this landmark Coronado realized the Turk was leading him in "the wrong direction" and reversed his course to a Second Barranca, where he made decisions to send the force back to Tigüex and to lead a group of horsemen north in search of Quivira.

Since the land east of the Llano is rife with ravines, the vague descriptions of the barrancas make it difficult to tie them to particular places in West Texas. However, Pedro de Castañeda had a green thumb (or eye), and the details he recorded about the displays of flora in some of those ravines converted them into trail markers.

It was June, and the observant Castañeda noted there were kidney (probably mesquite) beans, nut (undoubtedly pecan) trees, "many groves of mulberry

Texas: Endless vista on the Llano

trees . . . prunes like Castile . . . [and] rosebushes with fruit." He also described vineyards of wild grapes and reported that "although there were ripe ones . . . they made verjuice from unripe grapes."

This botanical evidence, as we shall see, supplied revealing clues about the valleys the Spaniards "passed by" in the summer of 1541.

☽ The Texas Route Mysteries

Since the 1920s, there has been a dispute in Texas about the location of Coronado's trails. In West Texas, Don Francisco and his companions described so few memorable landmarks that Dr. Bolton—and other Coronado aficionados—reached sharply conflicting conclusions about where, or how far, the conquistadores traveled in the Lone Star State.

When he surveyed the terrain in the 1940s, Dr. Bolton was rather magisterial in drawing conclusions about Coronado's paths. He made some major misjudgments, however, and since it is a trait of Texans to cast a cold eye on the interpretations of outsiders, it was inevitable that natives steeped in local land lore would challenge hypotheses framed by Herbert Bolton.

In my view, the West Texas chronicles are so incomplete and confusing, it is the better part of wisdom not to look for *the* trail but, rather, to ask: Where —and how wide—was the swath of country the conquistadores explored?

When the captain general wrote that he systematically sent ". . . captains and men in many directions to find out whether there was anything in this country which could be of service to your Majesty," he gave us reasons to use a wide-angle approach as we attempt to plot his travels on our maps. In my view, if Dr. Bolton erred about the West Texas routes, it was because he apparently felt compelled to be decisive even though the reports cried out that the Spaniards were lost or bewildered.

Dr. Bolton relied mainly on descriptions of distances traveled and prominent landmarks. This method worked well in tracing the routes from Compostela to the Rio Grande, so it must have seemed reasonable to him to use the same technique on the plains.

Bolton asserted that from a bridge the Spaniards built over the Pecos River at Anton Chico, Don Francisco went north of Tucumcari to the Canadian

River, where his force met the Querecho Indians. He next pronounced that the Spaniards ascended the Llano where today's Interstate Highway 40 climbs onto that mesa and thereafter marched toward Amarillo to a camp in the vicinity of Vega, Texas.

The paramount reason why there is still a splendid trail mystery in West Texas in the 1980s is that the explorers lost their way for three weeks, victims of the famous "blinding effect" of the Llano Estacado. Coronado referred to an interval ". . . while we were lost on these plains"—and the silence and vagueness in this section of the chronicles suggest that all of the Spaniards were disoriented.

In his book, Bolton first acknowledges the existence of this gap by admitting ". . . [they] wandered for many days over the trackless plains going generally southeastward." Then, with sudden strokes, we learn he is "certain" that Tule Canyon was the First Barranca, that Palo Duro Canyon was the Second Barranca, and that the Spaniards never left the Llano Estacado while they were in present-day Texas. Although it is probably a sound surmise that Coronado and his crew discovered the Palo Duro Canyon (now the most scenic state park in Texas) and explored in and around Tule Canyon—there is convincing evidence that the conquistadores did leave the Llano and did journey much farther south than Bolton suspected.

As a trail guide, Dr. Bolton has a springy step and takes his Spaniards to their destinations with military precision. He informs us, for example, that Coronado and his Quivira-bound horsemen ". . . ascended the Texas Panhandle west of the 100th meridian . . . and continued with a slight eastward swing through southern Kansas to the Arkansas River." And with equal dispatch, he states that Indian guides led Arellano and his army "almost due west" up the South Tule River between Plainview and Tulia, on to Blackwater Draw, near Muleshoe, up New Mexico's Portales Valley, down the palisades of the Llano Estacado to a spring at Taibán, and thence to the Pecos River near old Fort Sumner ". . . below the bridge that had been built on the outward journey."

Texas students of Coronado's journeys began printing their own findings even before Herbert Bolton finished *Coronado: Knight of Pueblos and Plains*. In 1944, W. C. Holden, a Texas historian, reviewed the chronicles, walked or rode over the same ground Herbert Bolton had traversed, and rejected

Bolton's conclusion that Coronado left the Pecos and marched directly to the Canadian River. It was Dr. Holden's judgment that the conquistadores hugged the Pecos to Santa Rosa, then turned east and climbed onto the Llano on a "middle crossing" Indian trail that took them down Frio Draw. That assumption caused him to conclude that Coronado met the Querecho Indians not on the Canadian but at the confluence of the Frio and Tierra Blanca creeks, east of Hereford, Texas.

The noted petroleum geologist E. DeGolyer was the next Texan to tackle the Coronado conundrum. He was the first to suggest that Coronado not only traveled much farther south but actually rode off the Llano before he turned about on his quest for Quivira. DeGolyer located the First Barranca a few miles southeast of Lubbock in Yellowhouse Canyon and fixed the site of the Second Barranca north of that locale in the "breaks" somewhere east of the Caprock promontories of the Llano Estacado.

It was, however, an imaginative Wichita Falls high school instructor who raised the most serious questions about the Bolton scenario. This self-styled trail detective was J. W. Williams. He developed elegant horticultural insights to support a theory that Don Francisco not only left the Caprock but toured far to the south before he became aware he was being led in "the wrong direction."

Williams was an amateur botanist, and his outdoor intuition told him the flora of the land—the pecan trees, plums, and wild grapes described by the Spaniards—might supply markers that would fix the southern terminus of the march and resolve "the Coronado tangle." He solved his "case" by studying the history of the native trees of West Texas and by compiling expert knowledge about the ripening cycles of wild grapes and plums in this region.

As a botanical Sherlock Holmes, Williams first ascertained that there were no wild pecan trees in or near the Llano Estacado. He then conducted an analysis that demonstrated that the westernmost county in West Texas with large groves of pecan trees (that is, the one closest to New Mexico's reach of the Pecos River) was Sterling County, just north of San Angelo. Williams next "drove a nail into a map" to tie the Spaniards to the ravine where he presumed they ended their southerly wanderings.

To support his pecan thesis, J. W. Williams assembled an array of horti-cultural evidence demonstrating that only near the latitude of Sterling County would one find wild grapes (probably of the mustang variety) "beginning to ripen" in June as Coronado and his men roamed about in West Texas. Here,

Palo Duro Canyon State Park, east of Canyon, Texas

he felt, was evidence offered by nature that, like a porcupine, would be diffi-cult to deal with.

Since this modest high school teacher first published his findings, twenty-five years ago, no one has disputed the conclusions he developed while he was sleuthing in the bushes, although his site on the North Concho tributary of the Colorado River is more comparable to an *arroyo* or a *valle* than a *barranca*.

Yet if Williams's evidence is irrefutable, it is obvious that he knocked Herbert Bolton's Texas trail thesis into a ten-gallon hat: He disqualified Tule and Palo Duro canyons as the two historic barrancas; and he established that the Spaniards were not only led off the Llano but actually entered the valley of

Texas: Tule Canyon, the "First Barranca"?

the North Concho River (a tributary of Cabeza de Vaca's "river of nuts") and intersected the path followed by De Vaca six years earlier. And, finally, Williams's findings explained what Castañeda meant when he wrote about ". . . the great detour they had made toward Florida."

To tie up his loose ends, J. W. Williams then proceeded to plot a trail he presumed the expedition followed on its way back to New Mexico. Relying on landmarks, he concluded that Arellano's Indian guides had him backtrack north to the Double Mountain Fork of the Brazos River, up that stream past Lubbock to the area where Yellowhouse Canyon tapers into a plains draw, and then back to the Pecos River via the Portales Valley, Taibán Spring, and Fort Sumner.

Williams made an obvious mistake at the conclusion of his paper when he undertook the task of locating the First Barranca. The chronicles are clear that the two barrancas were a few miles apart in the same botanical belt. Yet this energetic schoolman turned his back on the floral proofs he had gathered and announced that the First Barranca was Quitaque Canyon, a scenic jewel just south of Texas's Caprock Canyons State Park. This choice was odd because Quitaque is two hundred miles north of San Angelo, out of the pecan orchards, at a latitude where grapes do not ripen in the month of June.

Building on the basic data provided by J. W. Williams, the next West Texan to tackle the Coronado thicket was R. M. Wagstaff, a prominent Abilene lawyer. Wagstaff regarded Williams's tree-and-shrub evidence as "unanswerable," but he was convinced the Wichita Falls teacher was wrong about Quitaque. Wagstaff adroitly used Williams's trees and bushes to prove that the North Concho ravine in Sterling County— not Quitaque Canyon— was the First Barranca.

Solicitor Wagstaff's interest was piqued by facts Bolton and the others had largely overlooked. What caught the eye of this barrister-turned-detective was the flat declaration in two of the chronicles that when Coronado left the Second Barranca and set out for Quivira, he used a compass to march "north by the needle" to the point where the great bend of the Arkansas River begins in Kansas. Wagstaff reasoned that a hallowed rule of evidence sanctioned by the U.S. Supreme Court—and some commonsense calculations about the distance the conquistadores traveled in four summer days—would enable him to follow a line of longitude and locate the ravine the Spaniards described as the Second Barranca.

In a famous boundary case in the early years of the republic, the U.S. Supreme Court held that where a "known point" can be linked to a direction of the compass ". . . the dictate of common sense" is to "reverse the calls" to locate an unknown point needed to establish a marker or a boundary line. Using this rule of law, Wagstaff drew a line due south from the town of Ford, Kansas, to a ravine on the Elm Fork of the Brazos River west of Buffalo Gap —in an area equidistant from the cities of Sweetwater and Abilene, Texas. With a legalistic flourish, he proclaimed this was the site of the Second Barranca.

If one accepts the "Wagstaff Line" as being logical—and also assumes that Coronado sent his riders ". . . out in all directions"—it follows that the 1541 conquistadores effectively explored a belt of land at least twenty-five miles wide on either side of the 100th meridian. This means, in turn, that a large number of unsuspecting communities in West Texas, Oklahoma, and southwestern Kansas were in the path of discovery trod by Coronado and his thirty companions.

Counselor Wagstaff made one final point before he rested his case. To prove the Spaniards explored the midsection of West Texas, he focused on passages in the Spanish chronicles that demonstrate that Don Francisco's route overlapped Cabeza de Vaca's. Castañeda wrote: ". . . Cabeza de Vaca and Dorantes had passed this way." Likewise, Jaramillo mentioned that at one of the barrancas ". . . there was an old blind man with a beard" who "had seen four others like us many days before." To Wagstaff, these references demonstrated that the captain general reached the summer hunting ground of the Teyas Indians in the Colorado River uplands and were thus cogent evidence that both historic barrancas were in the Sterling–Abilene–Sweetwater triangle of West Texas.

Kansas and the Kingdom of Quivira

*I can remember exactly how the country looked to me as I
walked beside my grandmother along the faint wagontracks
on that early November morning . . . for more than anything
else I felt motion in the landscape: in the fresh, easy blowing*

morning wind . . . and in the earth itself . . . as if the
shaggy grass were a sort of loose hide . . . and underneath
it herds of wild buffalo were galloping, galloping.
—WILLA CATHER
My Antonia

WHETHER ONE IS CONVINCED that Vázquez de Coronado traveled north from Abilene, Texas, along the Wagstaff Line or shares Bolton's belief that the general and his chosen thirty angled northeast from Palo Duro Canyon, the Texas standoff ends at the Arkansas River. Both sides agree that Coronado waded across the river at the crossing where Ford, Kansas, is now, and the chronicles are lucid about where the Spaniards went and what they saw in the "province of Quivira," near the center of the state that is today the geographical center of the forty-eight contiguous states.

The confusion ended at the Arkansas because the view from the high ground on the trail provided instant orientation, and there were creeks and hills and small buttes along the way that made the Kansas countryside memorable. The Spaniards were now riding on an Indian trail that stretched from the Pecos Pueblo to Quivira, a tradeway that would become the most famous wagon road in the West three centuries later—the Santa Fe Trail.

Nature, imperious as always, dictated that, over a span of three and one half centuries, this particular patch of ground would serve as a path for Indian runners, for packtrains, for a great western wagon way—and finally for the steel rails that would make wagon travel obsolete.

The Santa Fe Trail was the first—and the most dangerous—of the trans-Mississippi trails of the nineteenth century. It was Don Francisco Vázquez de Coronado in his century, not westering mule skinners from Missouri in the 1820s, who opened this trail to use by Europeans. The annals of that romantic road remind us that, after 1541, Spaniards and Frenchmen followed Coronado's footsteps along that trail for nearly three hundred years before U.S. citizens appeared on the scene.

The conquistadores marched for three or four days along the north bank of the Arkansas River to its great bend. Here were undulating hills, herds of buffalo, and grasses that grew taller as the climate became more moist. After passing Kinsley, the horsemen surely stopped at the Pawnee Fork tributary, which bisects present-day Larned, Kansas. A small town that has an intense love affair with its past, Larned maintains a Santa Fe Trail Center museum that does a superb job of interpreting the story of that trail.

Larned is steeped in history. It has a knoll called Lookout Hill within its city limits, which Santa Fe Trail scouts, called "pilots," used as a platform to scan the surrounding grasslands for roving bands of Indians. And six miles west of Larned is an 1859 military fort that has been restored by the National Park Service and is now an attractive historic site.

East of Larned, the captain general led his men to Pawnee Rock, one of the remembered monuments on the Santa Fe Trail. On the rocky face of this minibutte, travelers—including perhaps some of Coronado's soldiers—carved names and dates that made it a priceless repository of inscriptions. However, unlike New Mexico's El Morro inscription rock, Pawnee Rock was not protected by a semiwilderness environment, and most of its signatures were lost when unthinking local folk turned that tablet of history into a quarry.

On arriving at the apex of the Great Bend, the ancient Indian trail left the big river and headed straight east past Plum Buttes (another famous Santa Fe Trail landmark) to fields along tributaries of the Arkansas River in Rice County, where the homes of the Indians of the Land of Quivira were situated. Juan Jaramillo was undoubtedly describing the feeder creeks of the Little Arkansas River when he wrote, ". . . we found them [the villages] along streams which, although they did not carry much water, were good, had fine banks, and flowed into the larger [river]."

Certainly, regarding the Little Arkansas area as the situs of Coronado's Quivira was established by a series of initial "digs" carried out over several decades under the auspices of the Smithsonian Institution. The Smithsonian's digger-in-chief was a Kansas farm boy, Waldo R. Wedel, who became the authority on Quiviran culture. By collating and dating a trove of [sixteenth-century] artifacts (including imported Pueblo Indian pottery), Dr. Wedel assembled conclusive proof that Rice County was the center of a sixteenth-century Quiviran civilization, which later disappeared.

Since the 1920s, no community in the Southwest has shown greater interest in Coronado's saga than Lyons, the seat of Rice County. With uncommon pride, the townfolk of Lyons have burnished our Spanish legacy and kept the flames of memory flickering around the Spanish pioneers who discovered their area.

Interest in Don Francisco and "his" Indians began in Lyons in the 1920s, when two country newspapermen, Horace and Paul Jones, envisioned a link between the Indian artifacts Rice County farmers were unearthing and the half-forgotten story of the trek of Vázquez de Coronado to America's inland empire. The brothers Jones were self-taught archaeologist-historians who spent their lifetimes enlarging public knowledge about the culture of the Quivirans and honoring the memory of the conquistadores.

The enthusiasm of these two men triggered the work of Dr. Wedel, encouraged local farmers to become sensitive curators of Indian artifacts—and inspired the citizens of their county to build and maintain what today is the best Coronado museum in the Southwest. Moreover, their interest in Coronado spurred them to write pre-Bolton books about the 1540 expedition, to inspire research in foreign lands about the conquistadores, and to launch inquiries that eventually produced the signature of Don Francisco.

Rice County's commitment to history and Indian science extends beyond the museum it supports. Local history buffs have helped Dr. Wedel demonstrate that the "council circles" arranged by the Quivirans were probably solstice registers. They have dramatized the import of fragments of sixteenth-century Spanish chain-mail armor found in Kansas fields. And they are now supporting a promising new line of research by the late Dr. R. Clark Mallam interpreting a serpentine intaglio construct recently uncovered near the council circles.

But how far did the Spaniards roam in central Kansas? And what were their impressions of that country and its people? The Quivira chronicles contain crisp insights. Juan Jaramillo, one of the horsemen who made the long ride east with his general, thought this area had the "best land" he had seen. "This country presents a fine appearance," Jaramillo remembered twenty years later, "the like of which I have not seen a better in all our Spain nor Italy, nor a part of France, nor . . . in the other countries where I have traveled in His Majesty's service, for it is not a very rough country, but is made up of hillocks and plains, and very fine-appearing rivers and streams, which certainly satisfied me and made me sure that it will be very fruitful in all sorts of products. Indeed, there is profit in the cattle ready to the hand, from the quantity of them, which is as great as one could imagine. We found a variety of Castilian prunes which are not all red, but some of them black and green; the tree and fruit is certainly like that of Castile, with a very excellent flavor . . . and there are grapes along some streams, of a fair flavor, not to be improved upon."

Coronado also sensed the agricultural potential of this region, for he informed the king: "The country itself is the best I have ever seen for producing all the products of Spain, for besides the land itself being very flat and black and being very well watered by the rivulets and springs and rivers, I found prunes like those of Spain and nuts and very good sweet grapes and mulberries."

The Quivira aborigines were friendly and industrious part-time buffalo hunters who cultivated maize and built thatched houses they lived in year-round. They were handsome folk, for Coronado wrote: "The people here are large. I had several Indians measured and they were 10 palms in height [about seven feet]; the women are comely and their features are more like Moorish women than Indians."

Rice County lies near a transition zone where, due to greater rainfall, the shortgrass plains blend into the tallgrass prairies of eastern Kansas. Coronado tells us that he traveled as far north as "the 40th degree" and spent twenty-five days moving among the settlements trying to ". . . find out whether there was anything beyond." Naturally, these words have caused speculation about how far east or north he went before turning back.

Herbert Bolton assumed that Coronado feared an ambush and opined ". . . there is no reason for thinking that any explorers were dispatched from Quivira, or that Coronado or his men got beyond Lindsborg [Kansas]." Nevertheless, the reported facts lend themselves just as readily to the opposite conclusion. Since the natives were not warlike—and it was Don Francisco's normal practice to send scouting parties to peer into the next valley or to search the horizon from the crest of the farthest hill—an equally logical argument can be made that the general was venturesome and sent horsemen out with wide-ranging assignments.

If one proceeds on this assumption, some of Coronado's horsemen may have seen Salina or conducted a swift outing down the Smoky Hill River and eastward along the Kansas River as far as Abilene or Junction City. And of course such speculation adds an element of suspense to the Kansas entrada by raising the prospect that one day some of Coronado's telltale trinkets will turn up somewhere east or north of Lindsborg.

What we do know with some assurance is that, after twenty-five days of exploring, the captain general felt the first winds of autumn, took a vote, erected a wooden cross at Cow Creek (adorned with a chiseled message that emissaries of the king of Spain had ". . . reached this place")—and then ". . . obtained a supply of . . . green and dried maize" from obliging natives and set out on the return trip to Tigüex.

There is a consensus among modern trail experts that, with six Quivira Indians as guides, the conquistadores retraced their steps to the historic crossing at Ford, Kansas. There, again, opinions diverge and present us with a final route dispute. Attorney Wagstaff, a devotee of straight-line travel, stated that beyond the Arkansas River they "went directly" back to their original bridge across the Pecos. Since he took the position that the Spaniards entered Texas on the "middle crossing" of the Caprock, he invites us to infer that they marched by Amarillo, went up the Frio Draw, and plunged off the Llano near Fort Sumner.

Dr. Bolton was also convinced the weary horsemen backtracked to their famous bridge. But since he adhered to the concept that Coronado initially led his army along a New Mexico reach of the Canadian River, Bolton construed Jaramillo's words ("At last we came to where we recognized the country, where I said we found the first settlement where the Turk led us astray from the route we should have followed") as meaning the homeward caravan moved straight to the Canadian ". . . near the Texas–New Mexico boundary."

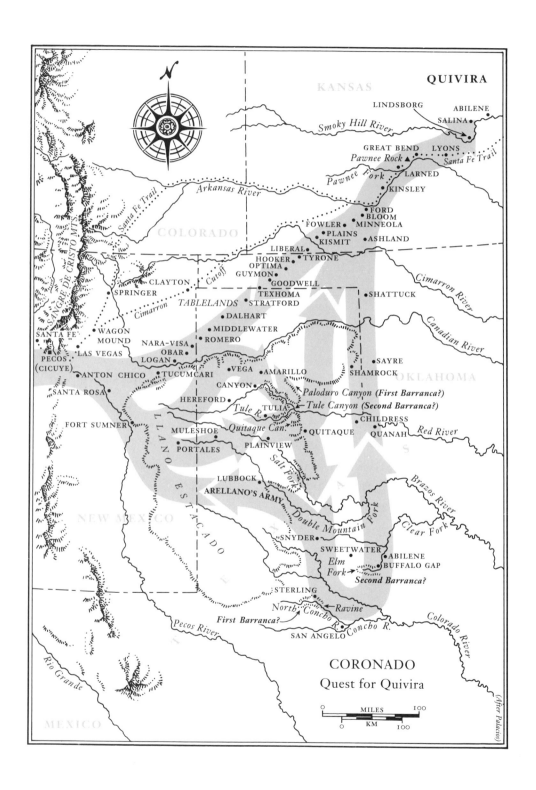

CORONADO
Quest for Quivira

(After Palacios)

As a consequence, in his book, Herbert Bolton makes the case that the path Coronado followed "raised the curtain of history for a score or more of present-day towns and cities" in Kansas, Oklahoma, Texas, and New Mexico. And since our historian enumerates an honor roll of the communities along that line of travel, it is appropriate to give belated respect to these hidden nooks of American history. Don Francisco, Bolton recites, ". . . passed through or near the sites of Bloom, Minneola, Fowler, Plains, Kismet, and Liberal; in the Oklahoma Panhandle, Tyrone, Hooker, Optima, Guymon and Goodwell can claim him as their discoverer; in the Texas Panhandle he passed the sites of Texhoma, Stratford, Conlen, Dalhart, Middlewater and Romero. Crossing the line, in New Mexico he brought into history the sites of Nara-Visa, Obar, and Logan, on the north bank of Canadian River."

Finally, after acknowledging that it had "been customary" for nineteenth-century students of the Coronado epic to presume that the Spaniards went back to their winter quarters via the Cimarron cutoff (a famous Santa Fe Trail shortcut to central New Mexico), Herbert Bolton observed that this route did not fit the facts in the chronicles and was therefore "manifestly incorrect." This was a blow to the communities that border the Cimarron Trail—a scenic pathway that ran through the extreme end of the Oklahoma Panhandle and by the colorful New Mexico towns of Clayton, Springer, Wagon Mound, Las Vegas, and Pecos to Santa Fe. However, these towns of the old frontier have so many stories to tell about their exciting days on the Santa Fe Trail that they do not need a consolation prize of tramping Spaniards.

The trip back, according to Jaramillo, was on a "good road," which saved time. He also intimated that some of the soldiers wanted to return to Quivira the next year. This was idle talk, of course, but there was a visionary gleam in the mind of the stout Franciscan Juan de Padilla. Father Padilla must have daydreamed of the hounds of heaven as he strode behind the horsemen, for what happened soon afterward informs us that he saw the Kansas landscape as a "wheatfield" of souls ready for a godly harvest.

Juan de Padilla's days on earth were short, but the next spring he walked back to Kansas and started a lonely mission on the outermost arc of Christendom that would twinkle in the wilderness for a shining moment . . . and then wink out.

The Long Ride Home

*. . . on the whole, the expedition of Francisco Vázquez
Coronado . . . no matter what the human drawbacks in
its operation and the fantastic dream which made it a failure
from the start, remains one of the most colorful and admirable
feats of derring-do in the history of North America.*
—FRAY ANGÉLICO CHÁVEZ (1968)

THE NARRATIVES INDICATE that as the Spaniards hunkered down for their second winter at Alcanfor, some wanted to return to Kansas and conduct another summer search for rich cities. Don Francisco may have given the impression that he was contemplating a second eastern expedition, but the "true account" he rendered to King Carlos in early October 1541 is the candid report of an honest commander who was ready to return to New Spain.

If one takes the liberty of putting words in Coronado's mouth, the somber, two-thousand-word letter addressed to "His Catholic Caesarian Majesty" is an effort to convey this message: I have been diligent and endured extreme hardships; I have led my men three thousand miles into this wilderness; I have done my best. But there is no gold here—and it is not feasible to establish colonies in this far-off land.

Don Francisco emphasized in his report that Quivira was "a very small affair" and that all the rumors of "gold and other very magnificent things" were the figments of overheated minds. The time had come, he implied, for the Spaniards to be pragmatic and recognize that this cold northland was not another Peru.

Coronado's letter to the king is a good index to his state of mind. The absence of any reference to a plan for a second sweep to the east, for example, indicates he was already thinking homeward thoughts. Moreover, his fulsome effort to assure the king that the natives he encountered had ". . . received no harm in any way from me or from those who went in my company" was a hypocritical, self-serving assertion that tells us Don Francisco had been sickened by the brutalities of the Tigüex War and was anxious to end his entrada.

It is also a good bet that, although no one wanted to appear fainthearted, as their second winter approached the Spaniards faced lean times that promoted pessimism. The expected supplies from Mexico had not arrived. Living off the land (which meant living like natives) was demeaning. And the suspicion and hostility generated by the Arenal and Moho onslaughts had turned the Spaniards into oppressors and reduced their contacts with friendly Indians.

But it was a riding mishap (interpreted by the devout Castañeda as an intervention by the "will of Almighty God") that started the chain of events that canceled the quest of the last great Spanish exploring expedition of the sixteenth century. The fateful accident occurred on a feast day in late December, when ". . . the General went out on horseback to amuse himself, as usual, riding with the Captain Don Rodrigo Maldonado. He was on a powerful horse," Castañeda recalled, "and his servants had put on a new girth, which must have been rotten at the time, for it broke during the race and he fell over on the side where Don Rodrigo was, and as his horse passed over him it hit his head with its hoof, which laid him at the point of death, and recovery was slow and doubtful."

It is difficult to determine from the chronicles what impact the concussion had on Coronado's health. We are told it was so severe he was "near his end" for a time, but the narrators do not mention broken bones, and Castañeda describes him on the homeward trail as a malingerer who "made himself sick" and "pretended to be sick." But if he was sick, or simply sick at heart, we know that Don Francisco was not too ill to manipulate events: He persuaded all of the "gentlemen and captains" to render "signed opinions" counseling him to order the expedition to retreat to New Spain.

It is also clear that a strong-willed minority wanted to stay "and hold the country . . . with 60 picked men . . . until the Viceroy could send them support or recall them." Juan Jaramillo, one of the dissenters, wrote that when Vázquez de Coronado "conceived the idea of returning . . . ten or twelve of us were unable to prevent [it] by dissuading him from it." The captain general was determined not to divide his command, however, and the return march began in early April 1542.

Military retreats are dreary exercises, so once the soldiers were mounted and had "turned their prow toward New Spain," each privately pondered what might have been and wondered what life could offer them in the future. Explorers rarely relish return trips, and as the Spaniards rode, downcast, by Acoma, El Morro, and the ramparts of the sacred butte the Cíbola Indians had named Towaya' lane, all excitement was drained from the scene, and their eyes, dulled by defeat, no longer studied the blue mountains and far-off mesas that had once been so enchanting.

Coronado, too, surely had many long, long thoughts. There were consolations to contemplate: He was alive, he would soon be reunited with his family, and as a devout Christian, he must have seen the hand of God in the outcome of his endeavor. However, like Job, he undoubtedly asked himself again and again why he had been singled out to bear the burdens of this failed venture. It was unfair. Except for the Tigüex fiasco, it had been a well-run expedition: The captains he picked had performed their assignments with dash and skill. And he had surely explored farther—and discovered a greater expanse of new lands—than Viceroy Mendoza envisioned. Why was life so cruel? Why was he, an invalid riding on a litter between two horses, at fault for not finding an Eldorado that had never existed?

There was plenty of time for trail thoughts, for the two-month trip to Culiacán was largely uneventful. Castañeda tells us that, at Zuni, "The natives kept following the rear of the army for two or three days to pick up any baggage or servants, for although they were still at peace and had always been loyal friends, when they saw that we were going to leave the country entirely, they were glad to get some of our people in their power."

Then there was a moment of excitement near the Gila River when the force intercepted a packtrain led by Juan Gallego ". . . with reinforcements of men and necessary supplies for the army" sent belatedly by the viceroy. Gallego was dismayed by Coronado's decision to go home, and he apparently emboldened Jaramillo's followers to make a final, fruitless appeal to the general that they be allowed to go back with the "new force."

When they reached Culiacán (part of the province Vázquez de Coronado served as governor), some of the men were home, and the expedition was disbanded. With the release of military discipline, pent-up grievances were also released, for Castañeda remembered that some of the soldiers ". . . began to square accounts for the arrogance that had been shown them by some of the captains."

After a rest, Coronado pushed on to Mexico City to present his personal report to Viceroy Mendoza. It was more than a meeting of officials, of course. It was a conference in which two partners could discuss a gamble they had lost.

Castañeda, always fond of recounting hearsay reports, wrote that Mendoza "did not receive him very graciously"—but there is no firsthand evidence to support such a conjecture. Don Antonio de Mendoza was a wise and moderate man, and it is logical to assume that he understood his expedition was a "failure" only in the sense that the glowing report of Fray Marcos de Niza had created expectations that could not be fulfilled.

The records of Mendoza's regime contain little to support the thesis that the viceroy was displeased with—or sought to punish—Vázquez de Coronado. Coronado's responsibilities as governor of New Galicia were continued. Mendoza gave him unswerving support when, two years later, a special judge was sent from Spain to investigate the conduct of the Cíbola expedition. And Don Francisco retained his seat as a member of the *cabildo* (governing council) of Mexico City.

Recent research in Spanish archives has disclosed that from his return, in 1542, until his death, in 1554, Coronado maintained his position of power under Mendoza and was even elected to the important post of *procurador* of Mexico in 1551. This evidence also implies that the two friends closed the book on their northern adventure and did not engage in recriminations over its empty outcome.

The decision to put this great entrada out of mind inevitably meant that it would be consigned to a hidden niche of memory where life's great disappointments and sorrows are kept. As far as we know, Coronado wrote no memoir about his adventures; and apparently there were no reunions of old soldiers that might have turned the glorious moments of the Cíbola saga into legends.

Vázquez de Coronado's health failed him and he died at the age of forty-four. His achievements as an explorer were unsung in his lifetime, and for nearly three centuries thereafter the documents that described those feats gathered dust in Spanish archives.

Coronado was the forgotten conquistador. His contributions to our national story were known to few until the four-hundredth anniversary of his exploring expedition, in the 1940s, brought him and his men out of the shadows of history and into a light where, for the first time, they could be recognized as dawn pioneers of our civilization.

Finally, one wonders how Vázquez de Coronado reacted to the supreme irony of his life: the circumstance that it was the man who stayed home to tend the store, his lieutenant governor, Cristóbal de Oñate, who became a grandee and enjoyed immense wealth. A few years after Coronado's return, Don Cristóbal and some friends discovered a great "silver mountain" at Zacatecas, which provided a vital second wave of wealth for the king of Spain.

Those Who Stayed: Coronado's Friars

But such was the atmosphere of the sixteenth century, an atmosphere supercharged with dreams—dreams of Indian souls to convert and Indian gold to explore.
— GEORGE P. HAMMOND
"THE SEARCH FOR THE FABULOUS"
Utah Historical Quarterly (1956)

THE CORONADO ENTRADA did not end when the last stragglers returned to civilization at Culiacán. An ecclesiastical postscript by its Franciscan friars enlarged the pioneering aspect of his expedition.

Vázquez de Coronado's martial authority did not encompass his Franciscan companions, and when he announced his retreat to New Spain, the friars promptly stated their intention to remain in the new land. Father Juan de Padilla, Castañeda informs us, delivered "a sermon to the companies one Sunday" in which ". . . he declared his zeal for the conversion of these [Indian]

Oklahoma: Dunes in Oklahoma near Knowles

peoples"; and it appears that he also tried to persuade some of the soldiers to remain and support his holy labors.

Fray Juan's decision was probably anticipated by Coronado. The restless father, the Lord's scout, had put himself in the forefront of the expedition from

New Mexico: Pecos Mission Church (1619), now Pecos National Monument

the outset. On the ground, "riding" shank's mare (as St. Francis of Assisi had prescribed), Fray Juan had seen more new country than anyone on the expedition: he was on Tovar's and Alvarado's tours—and then he strode all the way to Kansas with the captain general.

Father Padilla, an Andalusian who had arrived in Mexico in 1529, exemplified the visionary spirit of the first wave of Franciscan priests. The lives of these pious men were illuminated by the great doors opened to the mother church by the New World; and many of them believed they would soon locate the legendary Seven Cities of Antilia, a blissful utopia somewhere in the West supposedly founded in the eighth century by Portuguese Christian refugees.

New Mexico: Mission of San José de los Jemez (ca. 1620)

Some variant of this vision was plainly alive in Fray Juan's soul as he made plans to carry the cross back to, and beyond, Kansas. The only fear he felt as he turned his eyes eastward was that his God would be disappointed if he did not demonstrate great zeal in his missionary endeavors.

The second Franciscan who stayed was the elderly Fray Luis de Ubeda, a lay brother (that is, not an ordained priest), who ". . . wished to remain in these flat-roofed houses, saying that he would raise crosses for those villagers with a chisel and adze they left him, and would baptize several poor creatures who could be led, on the point of death, so as to send them to heaven." Described by one of Coronado's soldiers as "one of the most perfect religious in the world, because his life was a continual prayer," Fray Luis was escorted to Pecos, where he took up his mission with his tools, a small flock of sheep, and an Indian interpreter. What happened to Brother Luis after the army departed is a mystery.

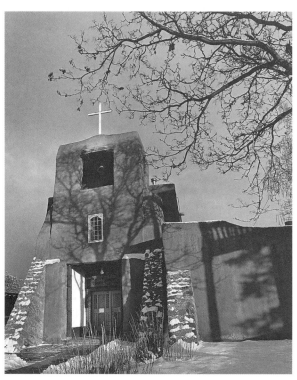

New Mexico: San Miguel Church of Santa Fe (1610), the oldest church in the U.S.

We know more about the fate of Fray Juan de Padilla, and one of the things we know is that his was a very ambitious missionary enterprise. The narrators depict Father de Padilla as a competent, well-organized individual who was both aggressive and stubborn. Thus, it was a very different Spanish procession of conquest that Fray Juan led back to Kansas in the spring of 1542. In the vanguard of this company of eleven were Coronado's six Quiviran guides, who were returning to their homeland. Walking behind them was a legion of the meek consisting of the friar, two Tarascan Indian *donados* (young natives who served as assistants to priests), a "free Negro interpreter," a mestizo (of mixed Spanish and Indian blood)—and one mounted European, Andrés do Campo, a Portuguese member of the expedition. Unlike the conquistadores who had invaded Quivira the previous year, Father de Padilla's clerical "army" took only ". . . sheep, mules, one horse, church ornaments and other trifles." The writers of the chronicles neglected to inform us whether Fray Juan also came to his pasture of Indian souls equipped with an adze and a chisel.

Vázquez de Coronado sent twenty horsemen to escort Padilla's party as far as Pecos, and they apparently arrived at the home country of the Wichita-speaking Quivira Indians by midsummer. But Fray Juan's ministry was short, for he was destined to be the first priest to win the palm of martyrdom in the American West. Castañeda related that this bold friar was murdered ". . . within a short time of his arrival" and intimates that he ". . . was killed because he wanted to go to the province of Gaus, whose inhabitants were their [the Quivirans'] enemies."

We have fragmentary information about Fray Juan's last days because the Portuguese horseman, Do Campo, and the Tarascan *donados*, Lucas and Sebastián, escaped and made their way, separately, back to New Spain. The story of Lucas and Sebastián is murky, but we do know that these resourceful acolytes appeared in Jalisco, on the west coast of Mexico, presumably after retracing Coronado's trail.

Andrés do Campo related a different, more daring, tale when he returned to Mexico City, sometime in 1543. Owning a horse, he was apparently emboldened to pioneer a more direct route homeward, east of the massif of Mexico's Sierra Madre. Do Campo recounted that he was held captive for ten months by Indians but escaped "with a pair of dogs" and threaded his way south to a Spanish outpost at the Caribbean port of Panuco (now Tampico).

It is fitting that the expedition of Francisco Vázquez de Coronado did not conclude with regrets or whimpers but with a dramatic martyrdom in a far-off place—and with amazing self-preservation by resilient men who had mastered enough of the arts of wilderness survival to find their way home across the lonely reaches of a new continent.

IV The Spanish Legacy

Our Lost Century

. . . the United States has little sixteenth-century history.
—J. H. PLUMB,
BRITISH HISTORIAN (1985)

IT IS PUZZLING THAT WE AMERICANS have ignored or disavowed a century we should view with fascination and pride. Events that changed the world occurred on our continent, and some who participated in those developments were the first Europeans to see our shores and walk on our uplands.

What explains this lapse? How did we lose an invigorating chapter of our national story? How can a nation that celebrates John Smith and William Bradford slight founders who preceded them in other parts of the United States? And why have we been so grudging in acknowledging contributions made in the dawn years of our history by people with Spanish surnames?

To find answers to those questions, one must hark back to the final decades of the sixteenth century, when Spain bestrode Europe and Englishmen began to nurture the ambition that they, too, might build an overseas empire. It was the hatreds evoked by the Protestant revolution—and the desire of the English and the Dutch to undermine the Iberian colossus—that cast the first dark shadows on Spanish character and gave birth to a "Black Legend" that Spaniards were innately cruel and depraved.

For readers of English, it was a single, remarkable man, the Reverend Richard Hakluyt, who launched a propaganda campaign that distorted Spain's great age of discovery and denigrated the character of her people.

☾ HAKLUYT TILTS HISTORY

If there had not been a Richard Hakluyt in 1590, it might have been necessary for the English to invent one. Having given England the stability and esprit it needed to fend off a Spanish armada in 1588, Queen Elizabeth put her subjects in a position where they could contemplate whether they were ready to reach for an empire. But the English had started late, so when Hakluyt began his propaganda campaign there were doubts whether his countrymen were prepared for a great leap onto the world stage.

A geographer before the science of geography existed, Richard Hakluyt became a herald of an English empire. A publisher of books at a time when books were rare—and influential books were few—Hakluyt printed reports of voyages by Europeans that opened the New World to English eyes, and he touted England's readiness to challenge the rulers of the Spanish Main.

The Reverend Hakluyt was an advocate who stood at a crossroad and persuaded his countrymen to seize an opportunity for greatness. Described as an evangelist-patriot of "immense persistence, imagination, and force," once Hakluyt perceived that Europe was at a turning point he made an all-out campaign for English adventurism: He beat the drums for planting colonies in Virginia, for expanding the British Navy, and for rolling back Spanish power. A visionary who saw the potential of the New World, as Europe's most successful political propagandist, Hakluyt conceived a program of action that became the agenda of the English crown.

Richard Hakluyt was a contemporary of William Shakespeare who used Shakespearean techniques to inspire his countrymen and to inject an adrenaline of daring into the veins of young Englishmen. Both the playwright and the propagandist were boosters for a greater England. Hakluyt's publications could have been entitled *Inspiring Books about English Heroes and Heroism*, for his skill with words enabled him to convey the false impression that English exploration ran on a track parallel to that followed by Spain's great discoverers.

All the Reverend Hakluyt had were a pen and a license to use the royal printing press, but he played a vital role in English history. His political ministry galvanized action on many fronts: Before his death, in 1616, permanent American colonies were planted, English sea power was growing, and his country had unfurled its sails and was moving toward an overseas empire of its own.

Hakluyt galvanized his country. However, what concerns us here is how he and his successors distorted sixteenth-century history and robbed us of the Spanish part of our national story.

As a self-appointed publicist for a greater England, Hakluyt faced two troublesome problems as he surveyed the events that had brought the dynamics of the New World expansion into the very center of European life. It was undeniable, for example, that by 1580 Spain and Portugal had already completed great epochs of exploration and dominated the world's seaborne commerce. And it was equally undeniable that England had been inactive during the glory days of the first half of the sixteenth century.

But a resourceful propagandist is not deterred by disagreeable facts. With anti-Spanish sentiment at a fever pitch in Queen Elizabeth's court, Hakluyt realized he was free to manipulate facts—and tilt history—as he pleased.

This resulted in "histories" that glorified English accomplishments, ignored Spain's climactic epoch, and spawned English fables that obliterated Spanish facts. Hakluyt had a deft touch. He altered the outlines of sixteenth-century history by muddling events, dates, and the deeds of individual nations. This flip-of-the-wrist technique so jumbled the two halves of the sixteenth century that Spain's age of discovery was only dimly discernible in his histories. Instead, there emerged the convenient concept of an ongoing age of discovery that English and other non-Spanish historians began describing as a "European experience" that was an outgrowth of "European initiatives."

In Richard Hakluyt's lifetime, this concept of a "European experience" became accepted as truth. It gave a permanent distortion to Anglo-Saxon interpretations of sixteenth-century events. For example, most English writers have depicted Francis Drake as a contemporary of the Spanish mariners Magellan and Cabrillo, who were dead before he was born. And readers nourished on Anglo chronicles were given the impression that Walter Raleigh was the first European to attempt to plant colonies along the Atlantic coast, even though Spaniards mounted more vigorous colonizing efforts a half century earlier.

The Spanish age of discovery is a reality: It is beyond dispute that Spain's dominance was so complete that, when the seventeenth century commenced, not a single Anglo-Saxon was living in North America. Yet the Hakluytian tilt has been so influential that today most maps used in this country attribute the discovery of the New World to the combined efforts of several countries. One measure of the amazing reach of this fable is that even in our time most Anglo-Saxons are convinced that their ancestors were in the vanguard of the great pageant of New World exploration.

THE YANKEE TILT

If Hakluyt and other English publicists started a process that erased a century of our history, almost all of our first crop of homegrown historians completed the burial of our Spanish heritage with a tilt of their own. The names of those New Englanders—Bancroft, Hildreth, Motley, Parkman, Palfrey, Jared Sparks—still resonate, for they started literary scholarship in this country and dominated our historical writing during the nineteenth century. The singular exception, of course, was William Hickling Prescott. Prescott was one of the first scholars to have access to sixteenth-century documents in Spanish archives. He understood the sweep and glory of the Spanish age of discovery, and the books he wrote became classics. W. H. Prescott not only saw the strengths of Spanish culture and admired the positive accomplishments of the conquistadores but he acquired insights that caused him to ignore the "Black Legend" nonsense. He was once described as ". . . the first English-speaking historian of Spanish lands whom a loyal Spaniard could read without disgust."

However, Prescott's New England colleagues adopted the anti-Spanish attitudes so popular in Great Britain and pulled the blinds on events that occurred before the English colonists arrived. To them, European "conquest" began with the English landings on our eastern shores and continued under the hegemony of the thirteen colonies. Even scholars such as Francis Parkman and John Lothrop Motley, who wrote about France and the Netherlands in their finest histories, echoed Hakluyt with diatribes that blackened Spanish achievements.

Another development that dealt Spain out of the annals of American history was the nationalistic approach our young historians took as they chronicled the events leading up to the American Revolution. With understandable pride, they wanted to describe the evolution of America's new democracy, and since politics was, for them, the be-all and end-all of U.S. history, they pictured the country as an Anglo-Saxon juggernaut pulling a new society westward into the wilderness.

To these writers, events that had occurred "in the territories" before they were annexed or admitted to the union were not part of American history. England was the mother country, and the events that paved the way for the English colonies were unimportant. Their outlook placed Spain's continentwide efforts of exploration and settlement in the sixteenth century outside the ambit of U.S. history.

A look at histories published in the nineteenth century by first-rank American scholars reveals the impact these Anglo-Saxon thinkers had on scholarship in our nation:

- The five-volume *History of the American People*, completed in 1902, by Woodrow Wilson contains not a word about Spanish pioneering in this country;

- similarly, James Truslow Adams's seven-volume *The March of Democracy*, published in 1932, deals with our Spanish ancestors in one sentence;

- in his magisterial 1933 edition of *The Rise of American Civilization*, Charles A. Beard devotes a few perfunctory pages to the age of discovery but provides no hint that Spaniards had explored much of the United States before English colonists arrived; and

- in a 1942 work, *A Short History of the United States*, the distinguished historians Allan Nevins and Henry Steele Commager set a theme in their first chapter, entitled "The Planting of the Colonies," with the sentence: "The history of English settlement in America began on a beautiful April morning in 1607 near the mouth of the Chesapeake Bay when . . ."

This is not the whole story, of course. Some historians have broken the choke hold of the WASP stereotypes and have begun to weave the strands of sixteenth-century events into the fabric of our history. For example:

- Commager and Morison graced their 1962 edition of *The Growth of the American Republic* with a preface that describes some of Spain's contributions to North American civilization; and

- in Samuel Eliot Morison's two-volume *The European Discovery of America*, this superb writer caught the incandescent flair of Spain's discoverers and offered unstinting praise for those Spaniards he admired.

☾ RECLAIMING OUR LOST CENTURY

With the Hispanic segment of our population increasing each year, the gains would be substantial if we had the wit to widen our horizons and pluck our Spanish century from the wastebasket of history. Who, one is emboldened to ask, would be harmed if our national story began with

Ponce de León in 1513 instead of with the incoming English at Jamestown almost a century later?

The Columbus Quincentennial, in 1992, offers us a splendid opportunity to gain a new perspective on the Spanish part of our history. It is true that Christopher Columbus was a native of Genoa who has long been recognized as the greatest pioneer of our millennium. It is equally true that this incomparable captain not only made his great voyages as a Spanish admiral—but also galvanized a second wave of exploration by his countrymen that, in five swift decades, produced exploits and discoveries that will never be excelled.

Columbus commands universal esteem more for his vision—and for the human endeavor he inspired—than for the landfalls he made on his four voyages. His legacy, so uncertain when he died in 1506, was given a glorious fulfillment by the Spaniards who finished the work he began.

He, and the explorers who surged across and around the New World he had discovered, altered the outlook of their contemporaries: They opened up Europe's static societies. Their individualism nurtured an idea called the American Dream. And their demonstration that churches, cities, and universities could be readily transplanted to the new hemisphere encouraged other nations to believe that they could achieve similar goals.

If we want to enrich our own history, it would be appropriate when we celebrate Columbus Day not only to marvel at the vision and daring of this hemisphere's patron saint but to simultaneously pay honor to those who first scouted our coasts and explored much of the southern half of our country. Pineda, Ponce de León, Cabeza de Vaca, Esteban the Moor, Cabrillo, Melchor Díaz, Coronado, De Soto—and all the other sixteenth-century Spaniards who paved the way for the ultimate settlement of our country—belong in Columbus's pantheon.

The deeds of these American pioneers resonate through the annals of our history, and the imprint they and their ancestors left on our culture is both permanent and profound. It is time to bring them out of the shadows and into the sunlight. They will add a special luster to our national story.

It would make our national stage more spacious if we reached out and recognized these "other" Pilgrim Fathers. Such a gesture would lengthen our list of folk heroes—and burnish an array of place-names that lends a lilt to the American language.

To be sure, such a reorientation would involve some lowered profiles and create a few pockets of distress. But truth often offers compensations that assuage pain. Would our self-esteem be diminished, for example, if we were to admit that Daniel Boone discovered nothing? Or to conclude that the country Lieutenant Zebulon Pike "discovered" in 1805 had been a stamping ground for Spaniards since the 1540s? Or to acknowledge that the self-styled "Great Pathfinder," General John C. Frémont, did not "open the West" but, rather, followed trails blazed by Spaniards and the white Indians who called themselves mountain men?

The story of the American frontier will have a different flavor if we decide to add the dash and spice of Spain's sixteenth century. And our ethos will surely be magnified if we have the *Mayflower* folk move over and allow the authentic first families of our sixteenth century to share their symbolic front-row pew at our national processionals.

Spain in History: A Search for Balance

The great majority of English-speaking people of the world today . . . have a deep-rooted feeling that Spaniards are a cruel people.
—DR. LEWIS HANKE (1949)

By the term "Black Legend" is meant the accumulated traditions of propaganda and hispanophobia according to which Spanish imperialism is regarded as cruel, bigoted, exploitative and self-righteous in excess of the reality.
—DR. CHARLES GIBSON (1958)

O<small>NLY ONCE SINCE THE INVENTION</small> of the printing press has a successful campaign of defamation lasting centuries been waged against an entire people. That nation is Spain, and that campaign of calumny—known to modern historians as the "hispanophobic Black Legend"—made Spaniards pariahs and demeaned the character of the Spanish people. This myth, I am convinced, has influenced earlier generations of Americans to cast a cold eye on the achievements of our Spanish pioneers.

With many European countries involved, the campaign that evolved into the Black Legend first acquired vigor in the 1580s in the Netherlands and in England when Spain was Europe's superpower. Rooted in accusations that Spaniards were uniquely cruel and stained with depravity, the prejudices spawned by this legend permeated Anglo-Saxon literature, politics, and the writing of history for four centuries.

Because England and Spain were protagonists in Europe's long and bitter religious struggle between Protestants and Catholics, beginning about 1584 efforts were intensified in England to inflate and inflame the Black Legend. Where readers of English were concerned, accusations were directed at the institution called the Spanish Inquisition—and on Spain's inhumane treatment of the American Indians. The Inquisition was rightfully condemned, for it embodied one of the darker impulses that caused Spain to retreat into a medieval shell in the latter half of the sixteenth century.

To understand the origins of the Black Legend, one must first fathom the fear and envy that gripped Europe when Spain was at the pinnacle of her power: The Iberian colossus had subdued Portugal and ruled a whole peninsula, her seaborne empire encompassed the globe, her ships brought a rich flow of gold and silver and spices to her ports, and sixteenth-century Europeans regarded her soldiery as invincible.

But adversity eventually overtakes all empires, and riptides were already undermining Spanish power in the 1580s. The successes of the Dutch drive for independence—and England's dramatic victory over a Spanish invasion armada in 1588—were signals that Iberian power was declining. Most of Spain's troubles were economic. She had squandered her New World wealth as the policeman of the Holy Roman Empire, and it was impossible to defend her entire empire against rivals who were marshaling their national strength.

The English and the Dutch exploited Spain's vulnerability by building bigger navies and by organizing private trading companies to challenge Spain's power abroad and on the high seas. These policies paid off during the next century, but it was another stratagem—a propaganda war to denigrate Spanish character—that provided quick dividends for the adversaries of those Iberians.

Words could be potent weapons, as men such as the Reverend Richard Hakluyt knew. Anglo-Dutch pamphleteering demeaned Spanish culture and aroused a hatred that encouraged patriotism and raised morale in these two nations. This innovative "paper war" developed a reach no one envisioned: The loathing it generated swept like a giant gulf stream across human consciousness for centuries and made Spain an outcast nation.

This campaign against the character of Spain has been shunned by scholars until recent times. The Black Legend has been so deeply imbedded in English thought that few have bothered to question its dogmas. But a reassessment has commenced at last—and it is not surprising that the initial impetus has come from one of Herbert E. Bolton's students, Philip Wayne Powell.

When Dr. Powell's *Tree of Hate* was published, in 1971, it was the first book-length treatment of the Black Legend in English. Written with wit and controlled anger, it sums up a lifetime of research and thought. Dr. Powell not only documents the sheer bulk of the anti-Spanish materials that poured off the presses of Protestant Europe but demonstrates that, for two centuries or more, "singeing the beard of the Spanish King" was the principal pastime of England's authors as well as her naval captains.

Denunciations from Protestant pulpits about the horrors of the Spanish Inquisition—and a cascade of accusations that cruel conquistadores had slaughtered twenty million New World Indians—kept the fires of condemnation burning even after Spain's imperial power began to wane.

It is ironic that, after his death, words written in anger by one of Spain's greatest bishops, Bartolomé de Las Casas, were the main ammunition used by the propagandists to demonstrate that Spaniards were inherently inhumane. Yet this same bishop tolled a bell for humanity that still echoes in this hemisphere when he presented his arguments about Indian liberty to his king.

Today, when Indians anywhere in the Americas want to appeal to the conscience of politicians, it is Las Casas whom they quote. It is he, not Cortés, who is honored by a noble statue in Mexico City.

Bartolomé de Las Casas did not start the struggle for a just Indian policy in the New World. It was initiated in 1511 by a Dominican friar, Antonio de Montesinos, in a sermon protesting mistreatment of Indians on the island of Hispaniola. Montesinos's appeal, which the eminent Hispanic scholar Dr. Lewis Hanke describes as "one of the great events in the spiritual history of mankind," was the first shot in a prolonged dispute between some of Spain's greatest jurists. Montesinos not only condemned the system of bondage (*encomienda*) installed by the Spanish but he rejected the assumption that New World natives were savages fit only for enslavement. The moral questions he flung at his parishioners—"Are these Indians not men? Do they not have rational minds? Are you not obliged to love them as yourself?"—struck a chord that carried across the Atlantic and into King Ferdinand's royal circle.

Montesinos made little headway in Hispaniola, but a more potent advocate, Bishop Las Casas (who was later given the official title "The Protector of the Indians" by his king), soon became the leading agitator for Indian rights. Las Casas, a slave-owning colonist in Cuba when his vision was illuminated, became a Saul of Tarsus who fought unceasingly for Indian rights during the last fifty years of his life. He scoffed at the argument that God had created Indians as an inferior caste: *his* God was oblivious to skin color or racial distinctions of any kind. To Las Casas, when Jesus said, "Go ye and teach all nations," he meant that all human beings stood on equal footing as children of God.

The culmination of Bishop Las Casas's work came with the presentation of theological arguments at a landmark Catholic convocation at Valladolid. It was he who put the imprimatur of the church on the humanity of the Indians —and even though the government of his nation failed to implement all of the policies he favored, the ecclesiastical arguments he espoused at that conclave add luster to Spain's golden age.

But what about the other side of the Las Casas coin? Why did this good man fashion accusations that became the principal ammunition used by Spain's rivals to rend the fabric of Spanish culture?

Today anyone who studies the writings of Las Casas that were used to demean Spain's character comes away in confusion, for the moral grandeur of his petition for Indian justice clashes with the obvious exaggerations he used to indict his countrymen for atrocities they did not commit. Yet it is clear that Las Casas engaged in demagoguery in an effort to win what should have been a brotherly argument with his fellow bishops. And it is also clear that foreigners later picked up words and threw them back at Spain with telling effect.

But, to be fair to Las Casas, one must put his polemics in perspective. He was determined to end the mistreatment of the natives in the New World and to persuade his colleagues that there were grave abuses. He pointed out that some of the Spaniards who went to the New World treated the natives like subhuman savages. However, Las Casas had a universal view of humanity and never intended to imply that Spaniards were more bestial than others or that Spanish culture had blemishes that made its citizens excessively corrupt or vicious.

Science now provides incontrovertible evidence that the acts of genocide Las Casas attributed to the conquistadores did not occur. His oft-quoted assertion that the conquistadores wantonly murdered twenty million natives and left whole valleys littered with human bones was, we now know, an outlandish declaration. Yet this atrocity story was the crux of anti-Spanish propaganda for several centuries.

We know this allegation was false because scientists and historians have used insights from modern medicine to prove what actually happened when invading Spaniards came in contact with the aborigines of the New World. William H. McNeill explains in his 1976 book *Plagues and Peoples* that it was diseases, not cruel men, that produced a cataclysmic mass death not of twenty but probably of more than seventy-five million New World Indians during the invasions of the sixteenth century.

Using new tools to interpret historical facts, McNeill tells us the deaths due to plagues in Latin America were "catastrophic." He also reports that in the fifty years after Cortés landed at Vera Cruz, the population of Mexico alone declined about 90 percent: from thirty million to three million.

Dr. McNeill is convinced that the final collapse of Aztec power was due to a raging smallpox epidemic, and he concluded that it would have been against the interests of the Spaniards to allow their native work force to be diminished. He likewise deduced that comparable disease-caused die-offs occurred in Peru and in other parts of the New World—and that native societies were shattered by these epidemics.

Common sense has always cast doubts on the atrocity stories used by Bishop Las Casas to win his debate with other clerics. How, for example, could small parties of Spaniards have mustered the means or the will to slaughter millions of innocent men, women, and children with lances and primitive guns? The killers, McNeill now instructs us, were those Spaniards who were unwitting carriers of latent diseases when they came to the New World.

The stature of the philosopher Las Casas, the champion of Indian equality, has grown over the centuries; but Las Casas the polemicist has been justly castigated. Even before Dr. McNeill's book debunked his atrocity charges, students of Hispanic history were criticizing his verbal excesses.

The early Spaniards who came to the New World were a cross section of humanity. No one has ever pretended that they were a company of white knights. While some, such as Pizarro, De Soto, Guzmán, and Pedrarias, were often ruthless and cruel, others, such as Cortés, Coronado, Balboa, Menéndez de Avilés, and Cabeza de Vaca, respected Indians and tried to avoid violence whenever possible. It is, as Bishop Las Casas surely knew, impossible to generalize about races or nations: Spanish people have always had the same human vices and virtues as other folk.

Coronado and our Spanish pioneers have lived long enough in the shadow of the Black Legend. It is time to judge them as the other explorers and settlers who came to this continent have been judged. We need to evaluate their conduct as individuals and weigh their performance as groups of colonizers.

Bishop Las Casas sought to measure the humaneness of European colonizing by the extent to which Christian precepts prevailed in the relations between conquerors and those conquered. But since there is no meaningful method to compare the pioneering performances of different national groups, perhaps we can assess the conduct of the Spanish pioneers by asking questions that focus attention on the outcome of their efforts. Here are some of the questions we might ponder as we prepare to celebrate the five-hundredth anniversary of the discovery of the New World:

- Where, in the forty-eight contiguous states, do Indians today occupy the same native ground (not merely a remnant of it) that was their homeland when the first explorers came to this continent? Are these Indians situated in a region originally settled by Spaniards?

- In what region did Europeans make—and keep —agreements that defined the land rights of Indian tribes?

- In which part of the United States did Europeans decide Indians were "savages" they could not live with and adopt a "removal" policy that forced natives to leave their homelands?

- In which parts of this country were "Indian wars" organized to drive out—or exterminate —Indians?

- Which Europeans crushed Indian religion and culture as "barbaric"? And which tolerated Indian beliefs and allowed natives freedom to continue their own religious practices?

- Which Europeans intermarried with Indians? And which valued ethnic purity and considered natives inferior human beings?

- And finally, which Europeans evolved a live-and-let-live policy that allowed Indian and Christian religions to exist side by side?

The questions go on and on—and each additional one adds a tinge of pathos that should give pause to those who are wont to judge others or to be influenced by legends that distort history.

The saga of Don Francisco Vázquez de Coronado is a statement about the Spanish ethos and Spanish conduct in the sixteenth century. Yes, and the story of his contemporary Hernando de Soto is another, darker statement about that same era.

Is there a lesson here? Does it say "Go slow" in forming opinions about pioneers? Does it say that one should gather all of the available facts—and study the lives people lived—before passing judgments on nations or cultures or groups who migrate to a new land?

Spanish Elan: A Tribute

. . . on the Southern voyages scurvy and starvation were commonplace, and very many, perhaps a majority of the men who set out on them never returned. What made them do it? I wish I knew.
—SAMUEL ELIOT MORISON

Confidence amounting to genius gave power to the conquistadores.
—PAUL HORGAN

A FINAL QUESTION that hovers over Spain's age of discovery is why—and how—in a short span of years so few ventured so far and discovered so much. The usual answer has been the one Bernal Díaz gave at the conclusion of his "true story" of Cortés and the conquest of Mexico. "We did it for God and for gold," the blunt old soldier noted in his memoir.

But this cliché is not the entire answer. There were other, more subtle strands of desire woven into the fabric of Spanish motivation. And these, too, should be examined.

The lure of gold came into the picture only after the conquest of Mexico. When Columbus and Magellan sought a strait to the spiceries of the Far East, they had no idea there were inland Indians who had stores of gold and silver. And it is obvious that many of the early conquistadores who regarded the Indians as primitive savages did little more than pay lip service to the missionary concerns of the priests who accompanied them. Plainly, many of these young Spaniards had more on their minds than gold or helping their priests enlarge the fold of Christendom.

What was in their cultural makeup—or in the situation the New World presented to them—that made them so restless, so audacious? Why did so many Spanish mariners sail into uncharted straits and oceans? Why did Francisco de Orellana turn his back on the new Spanish civilization in Peru and ride his raft into the jungles of the Amazon? Why did Ordaz, one of Cortés's lieutenants, climb to the 17,887-foot summit of Popocatépetl?

Why, indeed, did Coronado push on to Kansas after the illusion that inspired his entrada was punctured at Hawikuh? And why, after the gold glitter faded, did so many young Spaniards settle down to the mundane task of building communities on the frontier?

The God-and-gold formula is simplistic. Attitudes and outlooks varied— and if we search for the impulses that drove individuals, we find a mosaic of motives.

The friars, for example, saw gold as a snare and a delusion. The legendary Dominican priest Fray Vicente de Valverde was the only one of the 168 Spaniards at the battle of Cajamarca who did not want, or receive, a share of the fabulous "room of gold" gathered by Atahualpa's servants. (It was Valverde who gave the dramatic sermon on Christianity to Emperor Atahualpa moments before Francisco Pizarro gave the signal for the onslaught that toppled the Inca empire.) The friars were single-minded: Their eyes were on Indian souls, not New World metals. To them, the conquistadores were mere agents who opened doors to glorious new chapters of God's work on earth.

In a different way, it demeans the quest of the conquistadores to portray them as mere actors in a gold rush. Many undoubtedly hoped for easy wealth, but there was also a passion to achieve what Shakespeare called "the bubble reputation." Spaniards were anxious to leave an illustrious legacy for their families, so the prospect of winning personal glory was surely on the minds of some of the soldiers.

Bernal Díaz and others who kept, or later wrote, chronicles reveal that most of them realized they were on a vast stage participating in memorable events—and some romantically saw themselves as rivals, not imitators, of the heroes of earlier eras. This, of course, could have transformed young men and made them feel they were living in a world larger than life, where they had to summon hidden wellsprings of courage to face their destinies and, if necessary, die.

We must not forget that the fainthearted stayed home and that those who chose to embark on long voyages, or to go as adventurers to *tierra incógnita*, were bold individuals, mentally prepared to risk life itself on the ventures they undertook.

It was the Italian sailor/scribe Antonio Pigafetta who wrote that when he signed on as a member of Ferdinand Magellan's fateful crew, he was ". . . prompted by a craving for experience and glory." Experience and excitement were intoxicating inducements to young men living cramped lives in Spain's austere, small towns. There may have been dreams of easy wealth, but we can surmise that many were enticed by the allure—and the élan—of crossing great oceans and exploring unknown Edens in a New World no European had ever seen. One can imagine the glint in the eyes of those young men when they turned their faces to the west and made their decisions to depart.

And it should not be hard for Americans to grasp that Spain was a new country then—and that the achievement of nationhood often promotes a mood that says, "Now is the time to attempt great things." Once Columbus returned with his tale of a New World across the Ocean Sea, Spain's horizon had a glow that lifted the gaze of its leaders and stirred the blood of venturesome men.

It was one of those moments in history when windows are flung open and opportunity beckons to the adventurous. Yes, there was more than gold—and the prospect that one might do well by serving God and the king—in the minds of the Spaniards who went west.

Their feats reflected the hopes and ambitions of men who, on another level, were involved in a search for themselves. Unprecedented opportunities for independent action—for Spaniards trapped in feudal social arrangements to improve their lot or even achieve fame—brought a flowering of individualism in the New World. It is said that some Spaniards of that period expressed their independence by quoting this line from one of Calderón's plays: "To the king we owe our life and fortune, but honor is the patrimony of the soul, and the soul belongs to God."

But, returning to Don Francisco Vázquez de Coronado and his friends, one wonders how they reacted when, their entrada only a memory, they sat in the shade and reminisced about their experiences. Did they regret that those who knew little of their odyssey or what they accomplished regarded their adventure as a failure? Were they haunted by memories of Bigotes and the buffalo and the Grand Canyon and the high, clean silences of the mesas and the plains where they wandered in their youth?

Sometimes poets supply answers to such questions. It is our good fortune that one of our finest bards, the late Archibald MacLeish, became fascinated with the lives of the conquistadores and wrote an epic about their adventures and memories.

The protagonist MacLeish chose for his poem was, of course, Bernal Díaz, who wrote his "true history" autobiography to correct misinterpretations made by Gómara, the professor in Spain who had composed a pompous history about the conquest of Mexico. Here, as one answer to our speculations about the autumn thoughts of aging conquistadores, is the summation Archibald MacLeish put into the mouth of Bernal Díaz as he sat down to write about "that which I have myself seen and the fighting":

> *I am an ignorant old sick man: blind with the*
> *Shadow of death on my face and my hands to lead me:*
> *And he [Professor Gómara] not ignorant: not sick—*

but I
Fought in those battles! These were my own deeds!
These names he writes of mouthing them out as a man would
Names in Herodotus—dead and their wars to read—

These were my friends: these my dead companions:
I: Bernal Díaz: called Castillo:
Called in the time of my first fights El Galán:

I here in the turn of the day in the feel of
Darkness to come now: moving my chair with the change:
Thinking too much these times how the doves would wheel at

Evening over my youth and the air's strangeness:
Thinking too much of my old town of Medina
And the Spanish dust and the true rain:

I: poor: blind in the sun: I have seen
With these eyes those battles: I saw Montezuma
I saw the armies of Mexico marching the leaning

Wind in their garments: the painted faces: the plumes
Blown in the light air: I saw that city:
I walked at night on those stones: in the shadowy rooms

I have heard the chink of my heel and the bats twittering
I: poor as I am: I was young in that country:
These words were my life: these letters written

Cold on the page with the spilt ink and the shunt of the
Stubborn thumb: these marks at my fingers:
These are the shape of my own life . . .
                              and I hunted the
Unknown birds in the west with their beautiful wings!

Acknowledgments

ONE OF THE JOYS OF WRITING this book involved outreach that produced new friendships. Another satisfaction came from the opportunity to get acquainted, through their writings, with the minds of historians who spent years working in the vineyards I had to enter to gain insights into Spanish character and Iberian history.

Books written by the late Samuel Eliot Morison are indispensable if one wants to understand the sagas of great mariners and the significance of their voyages. Morison's two monumental volumes about *The European Discovery of America* (1971 and 1974) and his *Admiral of the Ocean Sea: A Life of Christopher Columbus* (1942) contain a superb reconstruction of the scope and drama of seaborne exploration in the sixteenth century (New York: Oxford University Press). J. H. Parry's *The Spanish Seaborne Empire* also contains a splendid overview of this seminal period of history (New York: Knopf, 1966).

The works I turned to for the big picture of Spanish history were *The Spanish Empire in America* by Clarence H. Haring (New York: Harcourt, Brace, 1963) and Charles Gibson's *Spain in America* (New York: Harper & Row, 1966).

The most incisive, informative book about Spanish society in the sixteenth century is R. Trevor Davies's *The Golden Century of Spain 1501–1621* (London: Macmillan, rev. ed. 1958). It is inexplicable that many libraries in this country do not have this exceptional volume on their shelves.

I was swayed by Cleve Hallenbeck's conclusions in his book *Alvar Núñez Cabeza de Vaca: The Journey and Route of the First European to Cross the Continent of North America* (Glendale, Calif.: A. H. Clark, 1940). I had a similar response to the intensive field studies that generated Carl Sauer's conclusions about the travels of Fray Marcos de Niza in his tome *The Road to Cíbola* (Berkeley: University of California Press, 1932).

Haniel Long's prose poem *The Power Within Us* was published by Duell, Sloan & Pearce, New York, in 1944. His book entitled *Piñon Country* appeared under the imprimatur of the same company in 1941.

My account concerning those who did not return with Coronado to Mexico was checked against Fray Angélico Chávez's *Coronado's Friars*. This slender volume was the result of original research supported by the publisher, the Academy of American Franciscan History, in 1968.

In addition to Philip Wayne Powell's *Tree of Hate* (1971; reissued in 1985 by Ross House Books, Vallecito, Calif.), my probing into the origins and impacts of the Black Legend led me to rely also on William S. Maltby's *The Black Legend in England* (Durham, N.C.: Duke University Press, 1971) and Lewis Hanke's landmark study *The Spanish Struggle for Justice in the Conquest of America* (Philadelphia: University of Pennsylvania Press, 1949).

History buffs who want to get involved in the Texas dispute about the country Coronado traversed will want to study Dr. Herbert E. Bolton's book *Coronado: Knight of Pueblos and Plains* (Albuquerque: Whittlesey House, 1949; New York: McGraw, 1949) and then consult the following three counter-arguments, which were published in the *West Texas Historical Association Year Book:* W. C. Holden's "Coronado's Route Across the Staked Plains," in *Year Book XX*, 1944; J. W. Williams's "Coronado from the Rio Grande to the Concho," in *Year Book XXXV*, 1959; and R. M. Wagstaff's article "Coronado's Route to Quivira: The Greater Weight of the Credible Evidence," in *Year Book XXXXII*, 1966. I also urge those aficionados who want to get involved in real "back-trailing" to immerse themselves in Walter Prescott Webb's masterpiece, *The Great Plains* (New York: Grosset & Dunlap, 1931), and J. Evetts Haley's superb *Charles Goodnight, Cowman and Plainsman* (Boston: Houghton, 1936).

Among the old and new friends who generously gave me guidance and criticism along the way were three scientist friends at the University of Arizona—Emil W. Haury, James Officer, and Bernard Fontana—who have spent hours and days over the past quarter of a century schooling me in the intricacies of anthropology and Indian lore; Edmund L. Ladd, a Zuni Indian who is trained in anthropology and is now with the Museum of New Mexico;

David J. Weber, chair of the history department at Southern Methodist University; Dan Flores, a history professor at Texas Tech University; B. Byron Price, director of the Panhandle Plains Historical Museum in Canyon, Texas; and Carolyn and John Sayler, two new friends who publish a newspaper in Lyons, Kansas.

I owe a special debt to Fray Angélico Chávez and to Dr. Philip Wayne Powell, who not only critiqued parts of my manuscript but served patient hours as my "instructors" in conversational short courses in sixteenth-century history.

Finally, I extend a special thanks to three writers in our circle of Phoenix friends who made insightful suggestions about the text. They are Gilbert A. Harrison, Peggy Spaw, and Joseph Stocker.

Stewart L. Udall
January 5, 1987

Table I The Spanish Age of Discovery: 1492–1542

Date	Discoveries by Spain	Discoveries by Other Countries	Milestones of History
1492	Columbus: first American landfall		Last Moors expelled from Spain (Granada)
1493	Columbus explores rim of Caribbean in three voyages (1493–99)		Birth of Margaret of Navarre, author of the *Heptaméron*
1494			Treaty of Tordesillas fixes line of demarcation
1495			Leonardo: *The Last Supper*
1497		J. Cabot (England) reconnoiters coast of Newfoundland	
1498		Vasco da Gama reaches India	Savonarola is burnt in Florence
1500	Codiscovery of Brazil by Cabral (Portugal) and Pinzón (Spain)		
1504			Death of Isabella / Leonardo: *Mona Lisa* / Raphael: *Goldfinch*, *Madonna*
1506			Death of Columbus
1508			Michelangelo begins work on Sistine Chapel
1509		Portuguese reach Malacca	Henry VIII king of England
1512		Portuguese discover the Spice Islands	
1513	Ponce de León explores Florida coast / Balboa sights Pacific Ocean		Machiavelli: *The Prince*
1516	Díaz de Solís locates mouth of Río de la Plata		Death of King Ferdinand / Thomas More: *Utopia*
1515		Portuguese reach Canton	
1517–18	First Spanish effort to colonize mainland of Mexico		Martin Luther posts Wittenberg theses
1519	Cortés: conquest of Mexico (1519–21); Magellan's ship completes voyage of circumnavigation (1519–22); Pineda: reconnoiters the Gulf of Mexico coast		Suleiman the Magnificent leads Ottoman Empire
1523	Esteban Gomes scouts N. Amer. coast from Nova Scotia to Florida		
1524		Verrazano discovers New York Bay	Birth of Luiz Vaz de Camõens, Portugal's epic poet
1525	Ayllón: up Atlantic Coast to Cape Fear		
1528			Paracelsus: first manual for surgeons
1531	Pizarro: conquest of Peru (1531–33)	Portuguese begin colonizing coast of Brazil	
1533			Birth of Queen Elizabeth
1534		Cartier (France): three voyages to Gulf of St. Lawrence (1534–41)	Schism between Church of England and Rome
1536	Quesada: conquest of Colombia; Almagro begins conquest of Chile		
1537	Irala founds Asunción		
1538			Hans Holbein: *Christina of Denmark*
1539–43	De Soto explores southeastern U.S.; discovers Mississippi River		
1540–42	Coronado: explores from California to Kansas		
1540	Valdivia founds Santiago, Chile		
1541			Birth of Francis Drake
1542	Cabrillo & Ferrelo explore Pacific coast all the way to Oregon / Villalobos: pioneers mid-Pacific route to the Philippines / Orellana completes two-year float trip down the Amazon / Cabeza de Vaca: 1,000-mile walk across southern Brazil to Asunción		Birth of El Greco

TABLE II THE ANNALS OF THE SANTA FE TRAIL

DATE	TRAIL USER	PURPOSE OF JOURNEY(S)
Pre–1541	Foot path: Pueblo and Plains Indians	Indian trade
1541	Horse path: Coronado's entrada	Spanish exploration
1542	Foot path: Fray Juan de Padilla	To establish Christian mission in Kansas
1542–1870s	Horse and foot path: Pueblo and Plains Indians	Indian trade and trade with Spaniards of New Mexico
1594	Horse path: Humana and Bonilla	Spanish exploration
1601	Horse path: Juan de Oñate	Spanish exploration
ca. 1720s–1870s	Horse path: Spanish "*comancheros*" from New Mexico	Trade with the Plains Indians
ca. 1740s	Horse path: freelance French trappers	Exploration and trade
1806	Horse and foot path: U.S. soldiers under Zebulon Pike	Exploration: military reconnaissance
1821	Horse path: William Becknell leads first U.S. pack train	First U.S. trader travels from Missouri to Santa Fe and returns
1822	Wagon road: Becknell leads first wagon train from Missouri	International commerce with Mexico via wagon trains begins
ca. 1824–1870s	The great era of Missouri–New Mexico wagoneering by Mexicans and Americans	Multiple purpose: international trade; military road; road for emigrants
1846	Horse and foot path for General Kearney and the Mormon Battalion	Conquest: the Mexican War

Note: In 1880 the completion of the railroad to New Mexico ends traffic on the Santa Fe Trail.

TABLE III MILESTONES: EXPLORATION AND SETTLEMENT OF THE UNITED STATES DURING THE SIXTEENTH CENTURY

DATE	EXPLORER/SETTLER	ACHIEVEMENT
1512–13	Ponce de León	Explores both sides of the Florida Peninsula
1520	Alvarez de Pineda	Sails across the Gulf of Mexico from Texas to Florida
1521–22	Gordillo and Quexos	Explore Atlantic coast as far north as Cape Hatteras
1521	Ponce de León	Abortive effort to establish Florida colony
1524	Giovanni da Verrazano (France)	Reconnaissance of the Atlantic coast from Cape Fear to Maine
1525	Esteban Gómez	Explores from Cape Charles to Cape Cod and penetrates the mouths of the Connecticut, Hudson, and Delaware rivers
1526	Lucas Vázquez de Ayllón	Settlement on the Savannah River by 500-man expedition abandoned
1528	Pánfilo de Narváez	Explores coastline from Tampa Bay to Galveston
1534–36	Cabeza de Vaca and three castaways from Narváez expedition	Long walk from Galveston across Texas, New Mexico, and Arizona to the west coast of Mexico
1539	Esteban the Moor	Discovers Arizona and travels to Zuni villages in New Mexico
1539–43	Hernando de Soto	Traverses inland across parts of ten southern states; discovers the Mississippi River
1540–42	Francisco Vázquez de Coronado	Explores from California to Kansas across Arizona, New Mexico, Texas, and Oklahoma
1542–43	Juan Rodríguez Cabrillo and Bartolomé Ferrelo	Reconnaissance up the Pacific coast as far as southern Oregon
1562–65	Ribault and Laudonnière (France)	Colony of Huguenots in Florida and South Carolina wiped out
1565	Pedro Menéndez de Avilés	Founds first permanent community at St. Augustine, Florida
1566	Juan Pardo	Explores sections of Georgia, Tennessee, and Alabama
1570–72	Father Segura	Mission in Chesapeake Bay area a failure
1581–82	Chamuscado, Padre Rodríguez, and Espejo	Expeditions into New Mexico, Arizona, and Texas
1585–90	Walter Raleigh (England)	English fail to gain foothold in Virginia
1598	Juan de Oñate	Founds the first permanent Spanish settlement in New Mexico

TABLE IV FIRST FAMILIES OF THE UNITED STATES

The Oñate Families:
New Mexico, 1598–1608

Abendaño	Lucero
Archuleta	Lucero de Godoy
Baca	Luna
Barrios	Madrid
Cadimo	Márquez
Carvajal	Martín Serrano
Chávez	Monroy
Cruz	Montoya
Durán	Morán
Escarramad	Naranjo
García	Pedraza
García Holgado	Pérez de Bustillo
González Bernal	Ramírez
González Lobón	Río, del
Griego	Robledo
Gutiérrez	Rodríguez
Hernández	Rodríguez de Salazar
Herrera	Romero
Hinojos	Ruiz Cáceres
Holguín	Tapia
Hurtado	Torres
Jiménez	Valencia
Jorge	Varela Jaramillo
López	Varela de Losada
López Holguín	Vázquez
López Mederos	Velásquez
López de Ocanto	

Index